Alone in a sea of normal

An offering of perspectives for sixth-sensed individuals to secure more ease, comfort and relief in their human adventure.

Dedicated to all the Indigo Adults who made it to here and now.

Truly, deeply and sincerely – WELL DONE!

ISBN:9798227851345 (Ebook)

First Edition. 2024

10 9 8 7 6 5 4 3 2 1

Copyright © 2024 Alyce Dylan / AD'ed Publications. All rights reserved.

Table of Contents

Chapter:	Page
Greeting	6
Us and them	13
Humanity	19
Living on the next wave	25
The Indigo Child phenomenon	29
What is the sixth sense?	33
Where are these six-sensed folk?	41
What is it like to be one of us?	47
What is it about the five-sensed world?	53
Where did it all go wrong?	61
More?	67
The path to joy and happy	77
Interpretation	91
Real-isation	99
Making Contact	101
Guidance for daily living	107
Redefining YOU	117
Someone needs the wood	123
Tuning IN	127
Understanding Frequency	133
Wave-forms	143
Impact of technology	155
The sixth sense and imagination	157
Mediumship	167
The God-thing	171
Is the future AI or IA?	179
Acknowledgements	188
About Alyce	189

Alone in a sea of normal

Hello.

Alyce Dylan

If you picked up these pages responding to some sort of inspiration – like picking up a random book from the shelves of an old dusty bookshop, or by feeling called to it in some way, then YAY! Ooooooo! What a delight! How comforting to know that something in you said "yes!" and there is definitely something for YOU in what follows.

If, on the other hand some well-meaning friend gifted you this introduction to a new way of looking at the world for sensitive, or empathic individuals, then it's possibly better that you go right away to the nearest bookshelf, find these pages a quiet spot somewhere and retrieve them one day, when they call to you.

If you are one of the first group, and we find ourselves together here now through some series of magical events, then I am delighted to find you, because you are just who these pages have been looking for, and with you they will fulfil their purpose.

Is there somewhere we can go and sit quietly together?

Oh don't worry about the moats, walls and crocodiles you have about your sacred self, I welcome them as a sign of a heart worth protecting. Take my hand anyway, and let us find a comfortable spot to get to know one another.
I am of course the writer of this message, or rather the liver of the life that eked these perspectives out of living this life.
I too am sixth-sensed, as I suspect you are.
Now in my days, I work with people like you, men, women, children, all of whom have had some level of struggle with 'what is', and there are some things I tell all of those who trust and come to me for guidance and comfort – and here I try to compile the perspectives I share with those I work with on their journey out of pain and towards joy.

Joy?!

And if that horizon feels too far for you right now, lets just go with comfort, peace and ease. We'll update the goal as we move deeper into shifting perspectives.

I have written this all down here and now, not only to have something to hand new clients who walk through my doors to get them up to speed quickly, so our conversations can be less about how it all really works and more about them, but because I've seen the impact that sharing this understanding can have in the lives of others. These understandings certainly changed my life for the better. I so dearly want for you the transformations I've seen through the eyes of those who have come to sit with me a while, drink tea, and make sense of the world.

Still unsure? Is this book really about you? Will it help you in your life?

Are you really 6-sensed and how would you know?
Doesn't everyone have a sixth-sense?

Well yes, in terms of the human beings alive today, everyone has the potential to have six rather than just the five senses. Some babies are just born with all six senses alive and kicking and most start out with the five, and encounter the opportunity to awaken the sixth later on in life. Meditation, a healing practice, a traumatic event – these can all activate the sixth sense. It is as different for a six-sensed child to be raised in a world created for and by mostly five-sensed society as it would be for a sighted child to be raised by a blind or deaf community.

The number of six-sensed children being born everyday has grown exponentially in the last 200 years and society has not adjusted to this phenomenon.

If you are six-sensed, and perhaps have been from birth, the following might apply to you:

Do you feel entirely alone sometimes, even in a thronging crowd? (In truth: Alone in a sea of 'normal'?)

Do you like time alone while at the same time craving deep connections and conversations with like-minded others?

Does life feel just too MUCH? Too 'loud' somehow, even when there's no discernible noise about? Have you felt the pure release of sitting quietly in nature, not a person around for miles, and you can finally be YOU?

Is there a part of you that feels unseen, and has perhaps lost hope in being seen?

Did you have that moment – somewhere back in childhood – when you realised that all of these other kids, these 'peers', must have received some sort of instruction manual for living that just got left out of your 'pack'?

Did you learn how to chameleon yourself into the world around you? Behave as they did or would or in some way that would be acceptable but really, most of the time you have no idea what's really going on?

As a result of the persona you created to 'fit in' – do you often feel like the authentic you is lost somewhere, abandoned? But at the same time do you live in fear of being 'found out' as a fake because you KNOW somewhere deep down that you are not living your true self?

Do you look at the behaviour of others and just not understand what planet they (or you) are from? As if what drives and motivates others is a complete blank to you? Even close family members seem foreign. You can learn the principles, understand the psychology, but still at some level, people in general baffle you.

Do you feel your way into a room, do you sense the shift of the mood of a room? Do you receive insights which are never wrong to go here or there or pick up this or that book?   :-)

Do you have a clear memory of losing respect for adults in general earlier than most of your peers? While they were still holding their parents on pedestals, did you figure out sooner that parents, teachers and elders in general lied a lot (while demanding honesty from you) and were for the most part hypocrites? Even if you didn't act out about this revelation, did you find yourself unable to respect 'your elders' that you could see right through?Do you self-isolate, as if you're wrapping yourself up in cotton-wool? And then have bursts of forcing yourself 'out there', only to withdraw again and bury yourself in self-comforting behaviours?

Perhaps there are behaviours or substances that have made it feel better? Something which distracts you from a world that is too loud, too abrasive and hostile? Perhaps you do now or have once overused those substances or distractions, to the detriment of your life?

And despite years of exhausting survival, there is still a voice in you crying out that this cant be IT! This cant be all there is – surely! And so you keep searching, in musty bookshops or down rabbit holes, for something or someone to explain to you why you ended up here, when clearly, this place is not your home.

Alyce Dylan

And if I told you you came for the fun of it now. .. you'd laugh and pick up the next book. So I will save that little nugget for somewhere down the road and for now I'd like you to imagine for me for a moment:

What if .... ?

What if I told you that there is nothing wrong with you?

What if you answered yes, even to ALL the scenarios I laid out above and I STILL told you that there is nothing wrong with you?

What if I told you there is an understanding of the world that once you grasp it, you will finally UNDERSTAND why it is that "people" don't see you, and why to you, the world feels so hostile?

Sit with that for a moment, against all the rejection, the hurt, the feelings of being unseen – brush those aside for a moment and consider . . . . what if there is a way to understand life and your purpose in it that would assure you that as a six-sensed, Indigo or empathic individual, there is absolutely nothing wrong with you? Would you be willing to take a gander down that view?

Before you reject the possibility out of hand, remember I have counselled so many, just like you, from exhausted and shattered lives into full thriving prosperity, and perhaps even more salient, I have lived this life, as one of you, for many decades and I finally understand not only why I came here now, but I've come to an understanding of life that allows me and others like me to live peacefully, gently, and compassionately.

Maybe my understanding can serve you too as it has served others. There is no barrier to entry here. It doesn't matter if you are from the USA, Russia or Africa. The same truths apply.

I also promise you common sense. A sensible meander through a different way of looking at the world. No aliens or channelling archangels (not that there's anything wrong with that conceptually but who knew there were SO many of them willing to take time out to chat right?   :-P).

Here, I will just share with you what I've come to understand about this funny old world and why perhaps we came here, now, in this period of history, and why that can feel so darn ouch! And if this view serves you, even just a little, and soothes your heart, then that will be enough.

Love. Always.

Alyce

Us and them

As a global society we've endured centuries now of division. Nationalism, racism, even tribalism all seek to divide humanity and direct our ire or antagonism against some other group of people. We don't have to go into all the motivations for this continual manipulation or the motivations for buying into this kind of rhetoric to make room for the possibility that the next phase of the evolution of humanity must possibly be the eradication of all this division and antagonism. Not in terms of a global 'same-ism' necessarily, but in the sense of understanding that at their core, all people long for the same minimums in this human experience and if somehow that minimum can be established for everyone, then that does not negate the drive for exceptionalism that individuals should be free to strive for so long as their striving does not cause harm – and in this realm of infinite possibilities, there surely has to be room to imagine a world grounded in both caring for people and allowing of supreme prosperity for anyone who chooses to pursue that.

I want to be careful here not to introduce into that historical narrative of 'us versus them', a new string – so please know there's no antagonism and division in these next series of understandings. It is important however that the six-sensed humans understand that amidst a lot of false segregation of society, there is an additional pertinent differentiation that it would serve them deeply to recognise and understand.

A dear friend of mine once told me that it gave him comfort to see the world as divided into two distinct factions: Those who held themselves accountable to a higher power and those who did not. I chewed on that for many years and came to agree, that there is a distinction – it's just not always visible in a world where fakery and dis-ingenuity are rampant, So as a tool to assist us in knowing who we can trust, it's really not all that reliable.

I heard the same philosophy espoused recently in a different way by a famous psychologist who said that the two types of people were either those who believed in God or believed they were gods, and I think I'll be chewing on that perspective for many years to come. However it is important that we are able to identify those that hold themselves accountable – authentically – to a higher power or a Divine force, because it is those individuals who will tend at least to try to act honourably, even when no other human is watching.

Understanding this division then, can help all people to manage their expectation of others according to what another person holds themselves accountable too. Either its an all-seeing, all-knowing Higher Power, or its their own Ego.

The understanding that really served me, when I finally saw it, was the distinction between individuals who are five-sensed and those who are now or have from birth been, six-sensed.
When six-sensed individuals begin to understand themselves as six-sensed, with all that comes along with that, and understand that most of humanity are still five-sensed, this understanding can ease significantly the burden of expecting others to be as kind, compassionate or empathetic as you naturally are.

If you are still asking yourself if you are really one of these six-sensed folk this writer keeps going on about, here's some additional clarity:

- Does injustice affect you viscerally? Do you feel personally violated by any injustice you witness?
- Even though you know that people lie, governments lie and dishonesty is rampant, are you truly affected by truth when you hear it? Do you perhaps get 'goose-bumps' or chills when you hear some truth spoken and just KNOW it to be true?
- Do you get feelings about people and situations that later, in retrospect, you validate? Even if you kick yourself along the way for not responding to that knowing.
- Do you often feel driven to drown out the rest of the world? Either through intense focus on one hobby or behaviour or with substances?
- Does the unkindness of others shock you? Even after a lifetime of living in the 'real world' full of villains and soap operas, does meanness still affect you physically? Even if you've taught yourself to try to ignore it or discount it?

You see the six-sensed are chained to the ideals espoused by prophets and messengers of God in a way that the five-sensed never were – they might obey a command not to behave in a certain way as a choice to be obedient – whereas the six-sensed are as injured by the act of causing injury to another as the person they injure, sometimes even more so.

The six-sensed are truly a new breed of human being and what motivates us, what drives us and how we live and think is completely different to how the five-sensed think and survive. Just as we are differently motivated and driven, we cannot understand for the life of us what drives and motivates them, and so too, is it impossible for them to truly understand our deepest thoughts and feelings. Even the most exceptional psychologists have thus far failed to make this clear distinction between these two groups of human beings now living on this planet – those operating from five senses and those who have evolved to living with six senses. They have finally allowed the label of 'HSP's'. or Highly Sensitive People – not as an acknowledgement of this evolved state of being but as a state of 'otherness', usually to be treated or medicated.

Right now society is so clearly divided between these two groups that understanding this division will change the way you see humanity from here on. It's a soft division however – as tomorrow any five-sensed individual might take up meditation, or start practising a healing art or have a traumatic event and their sixth sense might activate, so at all times the five-sensed have the potential to flow forward into a six-sensed human experience, but it is helpful to know that in today, no five-sensed human being will ever understand you truly, as a six-sensed human and even if you learn all the psychology of human behaviour, you might be able to predict some five-sensed behaviour through book-learning, but you will never be able to personally predict their next steps based purely on what you would do in their situation. We are that different from them.

This truth is fundamental to understanding why the world and other people often feel so alien to you. Understanding truly this division can be so healing for the six-sensed as they come to see that it was not their 'fault' that their parents, caregivers or teachers did not 'see' or understand them. It was an impossibility that they would.

So how did we get here?

Humanity, an Ever-evolving Civilisation

We understand that all life evolves and adapts as its environment does. Birds learn to congregate around coffee shop tables for food instead of digging for worms because life has moved on.

Mankind too has evolved. Outwardly we have moved on from living in trees to having wheeled vehicles to supermarkets. Inwardly too we have gone from tribal and solitary to nationalist and now understanding ourselves as a part of a global humanity.

We understand human existence as an animal-like five-sensed reality with a bit extra. Understanding varies on what that extra really is, opposable thumbs? Higher intelligence? Or a soul?

This is the basis of what we understand of the human experience.

But for thousands of years there have been those who stood outside of that generalisation. Those who either saw and understood more or who were able to communicate with unseen forces.

In some parts of the world these exceptional individuals lived on the fringes of society, up into the mountains or in isolation somewhere. Some were revered and held a special place in a tribe as they advised and guided leaders. For some of us they were a sage grandparent or batty aunt who would read tea-leaves. But always there have been those who just 'knew more'.

At some point in humanity's history, these 'seers' stood out as a threat to the ruling classes. A notable example was the successful opposition to Roman expansion by tribes whose Sages or Wise Ones would warn the local inhabitants of a danger to come and they would be prepared.

The marriage of church and the ruling classes then resulted in the shaming and outlawing of any individual that showed even a glimmer of unworldly 'sight' and so whole massacres were carried out to try to eradicate those who saw or knew more than they 'should'.

Humanity generally accepts five forms of sensory input:
- Light – Visible reflection of light
- Sound – Vibrations at an audible level
- Taste – Response from taste buds to mineral elements
- Smell – Detectable scent of mineral elements
- Feel – Texture, temperature

However, we know scientifically that there are other elements active beyond those on the detectable capacity for the human being. Both sound and sight we know are severely limited to a band of perception for the human experience that animals show us even from laymen's observation, are far broader beyond human perception.

But there is a growing number of the human population who will tell you of another form of sensory input beyond those listed above that is energetic. Quantum Physics explains how the whole of perceived reality is really energy, grouped together or bound in lumps to form solid-seeming form and so it is understandable that there are multiple frequencies always flowing past and around us.
Emotion is a vibrational reality. Truth is a vibrational reality. Patterns exist around us in all forms and those too create a vibrational reality that can be picked up on and predicted – even energetically.

Humankind is constantly evolving. Right now the scientist tell us that human beings are losing body hair. Since so much of mankind diligently removes much body hair and wears clothing, of course it makes sense that successive generations would grow less body hair. Bad news for razor manufacturers but accepted as a natural consequence of evolution.

Why then is there such resistance to the truth that more and more people are – from birth – being born with the ability to receive and interpret energetic information?

This opposition continues at so many levels today, although the war on the six-sensed was at some point considered won as society accepted the 'impossibility' of the sixth sense generally and anyone who demonstrated any of the six-sensed attributes was assigned to the 'lunatic fringe'.

And yet, despite all these 'cleanings' and manipulations of social conditioning, children continued to be born with an extra sense.

In most parts of the world, this is simply ignored or hushed up, the child is moulded into a five-sensed existence through poisoning (with chemicals), reinforcement of social norms or through fear of alienation.

In some cultures children with this 'gift', once identified, are expected to be sent off to learn to become healers or witch doctors. Either way, its a rare parent who would welcome the discovery of a child with 'extra sensory perception' and so for the most part, if at all possible, if this truth was suspected, it would most likely be ignored.

Recent studies now cite 15% to 20% of humanity today are 'sensitives' – which I suspect is very conservative as most six-sensed individuals are in hiding or do not acknowledge their extra sense, but very little is available to sensitive people on what is different about them, what they can do about it and where they fit into the ever advancing civilisation of mankind.

There's a lot of information through groups claiming sensitivity is a direct result of their group, cult or practice, but spread out across this world as this new phenomenon is, that simply cant be true.

And the language gets confusing! Empath, clairvoyant, clairaudient, psychic – and depending on the culture we're from these words can have very good or very bad connotations. The 'normal' world (standard people operating from the information received solely from their five senses) just doesn't understand us and until just recently, mostly feared us or thought our place was in fairs with crystal balls and tarot cards. Hollywood has done its utmost to shroud any extra sensory perception either in frightening mystery or skewed it horribly.

There were a few television series, decades ago now, where six-sensed individuals were portrayed living relatively normal lives, just harnessing their sixth sense to achieve goals or help others, but those were replaced with exaggerated dramatisations of individual who developed impossible abilities like laser sight or temperature-adjusting freaks that couched the dilemma – what should we do with people born with 'enhanced abilities' – and seemed to suggest this would be a significant conflict that would lead to global war. Oh boy!

On the one hand we can understand this as the creator of such stories, being six-sensed themselves, and 'playing with' their additional sense through these stories to try to make sense of them through art (comic books most notably), but one cant help but wonder if there wasn't also some social programming involved too, that tried to associate conflict and inevitable drama with anyone that wasn't 'normal'.

More recently (the last 40 years), those identified as born with a sixth sense have been given the name "the Indigo Children" – which, okay, at least isn't judgmental in itself but what does that really mean?

I first encountered the term Indigo Child at a second degree Reiki class. Someone handed me the book that evolved from the research of Nancy Ann Tappe who had been studying early childhood development for more than a decade (the 1960s to 1970's). She noted that year on year, it seemed that more and more children were being born with some expression of an additional 'sense' or enhanced intuitive abilities.

It was her tone I objected to most of all. The whole book seemed to celebrate the emergence of a new wave of humanity who she felt, would bring humanity closer to peace, prosperity and enhanced well-being, without a thought given to what it would be like for those six-sensed children to be raised by five-sensed adults in a five-sensed world.

Of course now I applaud her efforts and her quest to uncover the truth of what she was seeing, but then, with the scars of childhood still unhealed, I felt that the tone of her offering celebrated what I could then still only see as a painful past.

Living on the Next Wave

The problem with Indigo Children is that we know far more than what is said or presented as truth. Untruth tastes wrong, sounds wrong and feels uncomfortable. The world can be so loud and overwhelming and since there is no dictionary definition for what we experience we try to fit it into mainstream terminology. Some of us express how environments are 'too loud' lights are 'too bright' or environments are 'too much' but what we are really trying to say is that our sixth sense is overwhelmed. There's too much information coming in that we cant make sense of and to compound it, no one else seems to be suffering as we are. So as children often do, we blame ourselves, we preserve our relationship with our care-givers by negating our experience to ourselves and taking the blame. We must be 'too fragile', we must have missed a key lesson that everyone else seemed to have taken, there must be something wrong with us.

This internal struggle often causes us to withdraw, seem introverted or anti-social.

We see through fake appearances, we can tell truth from lies and we often know when people are ill. We don't understand until much later why people bother with the lies and the fakery and if we ever reveal our insight by mistake, we are either feared or medicated.

I was deeply blessed to have access to nature. For a time we lived at the coast, on the beach front and then I was informally adopted by a friend of my grandmother who had a second home in a small village in the countryside where the world was quiet. The village residents were mostly elderly and so less taken with pretence. My 'adoptive' mother was a pure spirit with strong spiritual values and she did not lie. She was honest, authentic and very loving. My time with her showed me life could be bearable.

Back with my biological parent and step-parent, life was a raging inferno of addiction, passion, lust and lies – but it was my 'adoptive' parents that helped me to see that. Without the kind gentleness of my 'volunteer' parents, I have no doubt I would not be sitting here writing this all down today.

Like 19 out of every 20 of us Indigo Children, I would have opted out before growing into adulthood.

I lived the chaos of the Indigo Child. I walked the earth raw and exposed to every passing despair, every feeling of distrust and pain wounded me too. I always saw what was really going on, but learnt early on not to let on that I knew.

At school I was the child everyone came to with their pains and confusion.

I counselled the broken-hearted and the misfits but also the popular kids in their romantic entanglements. I helped children find ways to talk to their parents or teachers but the older I got, the less tolerance I had for wrongness.

I challenged lies, teachers self-aggrandising intentions and ignorant fanaticism. I may have had a much harder time of it in my school years without my ability to score well on every test and in all subjects.

I was an anomaly. Not a trouble-maker exactly, but capable at any moment of becoming one when faced with injustice or dishonesty. Depending on their own personal integrity, teachers either loved or hated me for it. So, I got by.

There was no widely accepted name for what I was back then. At age five I awoke screaming shouting for my biological and step parent to go and help Granny (who lived with us), because she was hurt. They reassured me saying that I had just had a nightmare and to go back to sleep.

Then the phone rang and it was the hospital letting them know that Gran had been in an accident and had been rushed to hospital.

People looked at me differently from then on, but the incident was never mentioned again.

I've known others who were discovered young and hauled into seances regularly as mediums, which caused just as much damage as they lost years of normal development to being a channel for others to satiate their need to pass messages along to loved ones.

As Indigo-born we all wear some kind of damage. Not being seen truly, not understood and seeing layers of human behaviour that our young minds cant possibly process – all glossed over by inauthenticity that feels like sandpaper to our very being.

No wonder we withdraw!

Indigo's are natural introverts, not because we're shy or reserved, but because we cant take all the nonsense of 'out there'. The fake smiles, the empty platitudes are seen for what they are while the adults about us espouse honesty and a litany of virtues that they themselves seldom inhabit.

But there is nothing wrong with us. It is simply a shift in the world that we are caught on the hump of, we are the trailblazers of a new kind of human being, and our withdrawal inwards or to the fringes of humanity does not serve us or the world. Humanity is evolving, and we are the leading edge of that evolution.

The Indigo child phenomenon

The Indigo Child phenomenon was presented as the next wave of the evolution of mankind where we are learning to receive information – not just in manifested form that you can see, hear, taste or touch, but in energetic form from our surroundings, our environment and from the people around us – both physical and non.
    The harsh truth is that mankind is not in stark need of a new breed of people who can leap tall buildings or shoot lasers out their eyes or even cloud-surf. What mankind really needs right now is the ability to distinguish truth from falsehood and access guidance from multiple directions in order to make better informed choices.

But it's been a few generations now since the "Indigo Child" research was published, and some of us from the 60's and 70's who form a part of this new wave of mankind have survived – unmedicated, usually withdrawn and with a broad spectrum of coping mechanisms – some of us even healthy. And it falls to us now to prepare the way for future generations of Indigo Children, so they don't need to endure what we did. And we do that by stepping into our true selves, understanding how and why we are different, and living our truth anyway – as more and more six-sensed individuals are now, across the planet, even if they don't know that they are part of this new version of humanity.

The world really does need us you see. While now we are a small voice in the dark, clinging to any small vestige of self-acceptance, things are getting better. The formalised 'medical community' and its Rockerfeller-manipulated origins is losing ground and the world is turning back to the truth of natural health, wholistic healing and a focus on wellness instead of illness and with that, we can chance an emergence from the shadows without the fear of being locked away or medicated just because we know what their intentions are, or how they really feel or if they just told the truth or not. Or indeed what Aunt Hilda has to say about growing petunias – even though she withdrew her focus from human form a decade ago.

There is space opening up for us now, out here amongst the 'normals', and in claiming the space with confidence and self-acceptance we heal ourselves, our communities and ultimately our world.

But first we must free ourselves of the perception created by the five-sensed about what our abilities or senses really are. There are no boogie-men hiding under our bed feeding us nightmares, there is no alien beaming messages down to our fillings.

Its not even all that dramatic – well not for us that are living it. So, okay, we know who is lying and we know who is honest. But that doesn't mean we're going to go about pointing out to anyone speaking untruths that they are 'liars!'. There's a way to go before most of us are confident enough in what we know to make any sort of pronouncement. But what is dramatically urgent is for those of us that have survived to adulthood to LIVE our truth, authentically and visibly, so that others feel less ashamed to do the same.

Perception is our greatest obstacle, with Hollywood having blown up the concept of additional abilities and language having no words we can accurately use for what we experience, so we tend to employ vagueities like 'otherness' and 'sense' when what we really need is new verbs and adjectives for what we experience. Trying to bend the perception of three dimensional people around five dimensional concepts is challenging – especially when you have limited time before they reach for the phone to call the men in the little white van to take you away to padded comfort.

So many of us learnt early to be quiet. To hide our senses. If not directly then indirectly from the judgements we overheard of others we learnt to doubt our sanity, became convinced of our brokenness and for the most part withdrew from others. If not actually then emotionally, with no-one ever knowing or understanding our true selves.

That needs to be given the space to change, and in some ways social media has allowed us room to identify others like ourselves. Some genuine, some attention-seeking, but its no longer a death-sentence in this world to be different and so there is an opportunity today, for us to reach a new understanding of ourselves and for humanity to understand how it is evolving.

So far, most of the research on our 'kind' was done by five-sensed 'normals', people who could only speculate what it was to live inside a mind saturated with incoming energetic data 24/7. What lies ahead of us when six-sensed people like ourselves begin exploring this sixth sense and what it could be capable of, out of genuine curiosity and a hunger for truth, rather than to try to harness the sixth sense for the war machine, is impossible to fathom from here, but it feels pregnant with exciting possibilities.

So what exactly IS the sixth sense?

Of course one doesn't have to speak to 'dead people' or be inflicted with sporadic telepathy to be a six-sensed individual! Because of the taboos around the subject of the sixth sense wild language and strange understandings have filled the void and created much confusion.

The sixth sense is nothing to be afraid of, despite years of social programming to make everyone fear it, it is completely responsive to choice. This is after all OUR human experience and our senses are responsive – even at a subconscious level – to our preferences.

So what IS the sixth sense and do we have to wear caftans and learn the guitar now?

Of course not! Unless of course you'd like to. :-)

We understand the operation of our five senses as we've been taught them in school. Our eyes allow us to see, our ears to hear, our skin and nervous system to feel, our tongues and nose to some extent to taste and nose primarily to smell.

But we also use some of that terminology interchangeably for emotional experience, so in some small way we've already moved 'sense' beyond the purely physical realm in our language. So you can 'touch' someone, emotionally, or you can 'see' a concept when its explained. Its clear that we only have the apparatus we know of (eyes ears etc), so how is it that there is another sense if there is no other organ?

It's really all about vibration however. We now know this from the field of sciences that light itself is merely a frequency that our eyes interpret as sight. The same applies for all the five senses, that vibration or frequency is captured through receptors and interpreted into a grid of 'knowing'.

We even know that our range is limited. That dogs, for example, can hear a broader range of frequencies than the average human being and so that leads us to an understanding that there could be a whole lot more going on out there than we can be aware of with our limited apparatus.

The sixth sense is merely the ability to gather an additional stream of information, which we then interpret through our existing pathways. I can accept for now – even though I have no direct confirmation of this – that our pineal gland has the highest vibration of any organ in our body and therefore is closest in frequency to higher energies. So it is reasonable to assume for now that it is our pineal gland that 'receives' this energetic information and then passes that information on for translation to our other pathways already in place.

'Seeing' has always been strongest for me. When you read a book or a story and 'see' it play out in your mind as you read, that aspect of what has always been assigned to the 'imagination' is a facility than can be harnessed to process information received by the sixth sense. It's really the same function, in reading or hearing you receive information that you project, in your mind, onto a screen that only you can 'see', as a part of the experience of receiving information and interpreting it.

Others can 'hear' information, but most commonly, people 'feel' the rightness or wrongness of something.

There are names for many of the pathways of interpretation – Clairvoyance, clairaudience, clairsentience etc, but all that changes is the pathways we use to interpret the additional information we are receiving.

I don't like clairaudience particularly. To stand alone in a room and have the experience of another voice there makes me uncomfortable, so I choose to allow that pathway only when absolutely necessary. Most people's pathways evolve naturally, they just tend to develop whatever is the most comfortable processing pathways for them.

This doesn't mean we cant evolve other pathways, but I don't see why we would need to – if we are receiving and processing information through a pathway that works, why would we want to work at harnessing a different one? Its not the pathways that matter anyway, it's how the information gets interpreted once its received that is important.

For many people clairsentience is the most comfortable, just KNOWING. Just knowing which road to turn down or knowing to call home or get in touch with this or that friend. It's unobtrusive and comes with less frightening possibilities.

A lot has been written and offered about these various pathways and there are courses to enhance one or many of the pathways of interpretation so I wont focus on those – what I want to be clear on is that it doesn't matter. The important part is the information being received, and then hopefully being accurately translated into some form of intelligence that is usable – and this is where things can go horribly awry.

Imagine a radio for example. It receives a signal and translates that signal into sound. Ideally that sound is clear and intelligible. But not always. Radios can be finicky and you need to tune to the signal so precisely to get a clear result. Any interference in the middle, and you end up with annoying glitches.

The first thing to bear in mind is that like physical sight or hearing, your sixth sense is primarily for YOU. To guide YOUR life experience. It can be an invaluable tool in navigating this human experience, and when you can stay out of the way of the information you are receiving, it can help you delightfully through your days. But even in entirely personal application, there will be interference.

Many of us will have had the experience of driving towards a location, and our mind tells us that x is the quickest way to go but our 'knowing' tells us to take the other way. After ignoring our inner knowing a few times and getting mired behind an accident or road-works a few times, we begin to trust our knowing more and more.

As a new field of human experience however, this is mostly unchartered territory, and people are flying off on tangents in this unexplored field making it more challenging for others to be willing to explore on their own.

Our personal preferences play into the art of interpretation of energy too, so the information can be distorted when it hits a hard-wired set of beliefs or prejudices.

One clear example of interpretation going horribly wrong is what many people cling to as proof of reincarnation, when children describe scenes or places to which they've never been in this lifetime. The assumption is made that they MUST be the returned spirit of Auntie Betty whose house they just described so accurately.

But really, in receiving information or communication from those who have abandoned their physical bodies, we also get to share their memories and experiences, so those children are more likely receiving memories from souls who have passed beyond the veil of this life and when they describe what they are 'seeing' from the other soul's memory, people jump on the idea that this is the soul of that person, returned.

Reincarnation as it is popularly touted today is not what happens at all. Life always moves forward, never backward and so while our path to this manifestation into human form took us through eons manifesting rocks and plants as well as various other living things, this one human experience is it for this cycle of life. We go ON from here to higher and higher vibrational states, but imagining that we return here over and over would be like idealising sending a child repeatedly to grade six over and over again. This is but one phase, one step. Dense with learning and experience and vital in our personal development but we will do this once.

And then we will BE Aunt Betty or Uncle Terry, sharing our experiences and memories with those who come after us as we clear up any damage we inflicted in our ancestral lines and guide those we can to better lives.

But you don't have to have a single experience with a soul who has passed on as a six-sensed human, if you choose not to. It's likely you will receive impulses and information from them anyway, but it can be as simple as receiving a thought. Nothing frightening at all.

I call those I travel about with, those unseen souls who accompany us through our days 'faeries'. They are certainly not 'dead' people, being so very much alive and the word 'ghost' has so many unpleasant associations which really are not appropriate.

My grandmother was six-sensed. Her husband had passed on long before I was born but Gran maintained an active and healthy marriage to her late husband right up to her own passing.

We would often walk in on Gran sharing the news of the day with Grampa – and she had a practice of going out into the garden and having active conversations, seemingly on her own.

The family came to say that Granny was in the garden "talking to the faeries" – I knew she was having conversations with either Grampa or some other unseen soul. So for me it fits to call those unseen souls that accompany us through our days and advise us when we ask, faeries.

I mean no offence to those who believe in little winged people – like most six-sensed terminology I've had to co-opt this one from public parlance, but I also make room for the possibility that there could be some truth here to delve into that could explain the origins of what people once understood as little 'winged people'.

In my days with my 'faeries', I have access to information I have never been exposed to in the years of human manifestation. I don't consider myself a great cook for example, I can whip up an omelette or prepare a roast but I'm no Jamie Oliver, nor do I have the passion for it.

One of my faeries however IS a great cook. I call him Dieter, while I'm sure that wasn't really his name. He feels like he comes from Belgium or somewhere in that region of Europe. I can be heard often arguing with him in the kitchen: "You want to put what in that? Surely not!" They are empty arguments though because I follow his guidance more often than not and so these hands have seemingly created some culinary marvels – although I always give him the credit.

Cars and parking are another faerie's domain and another handles outfits. Clothing bores me and it works for me to have a picture of what to wear today already in my mind when I get up. I've also learnt that if I am prompted to take a coat, even if it seems sunny out, there will be occasion to use it.

Now one doesn't have to go so deeply into the origins of knowing, you don't have to meet the faeries prompting the information – your sixth-sense will simply receive the guidance and if you act on it, you will have helpers everywhere you go.

We are therefore only ever alone when we choose to be, when we cut ourselves off or disconnect as far as we can from our sixth-sense. Unfortunately the impulse to cut ourselves off, as children, when all the incoming information is so overwhelming and makes us feel 'abnormal' is strong, and we may have gotten pretty good at it by adulthood. But if we are to live the life we came here to live, we must start here, to unlock what we have shut away and safely, and gently, begin to step into our authentic selves.

Where are these six-sensed folk?

So through this perspective, humanity as it is today is comprised of humans who navigate life with five or six senses. The five-sensed or 'normals' have been the dominant version of human experience for thousands of years and now – particularly in the last 200 or so years, the tide is turning.

As the research in the Indigo Child books outlines, more and more children are being born with six rather than the standard five senses and in today's world, it's far less simple a thing than it may have been 400 years ago. Then, there were village elders, medicine people or healers who would mentor the newly discovered six-senser, but those models are for the most part long gone. So now what? What is a six-sensed child to do with all the information they are receiving today?

As described earlier, they withdraw, self-isolate or try to tune out their sixth sense. Sadly, research also shows us that only 19 out of 20 'HSP's' or Indigo Children choose not to make it to adulthood because its really not an easy road.

It's is interesting to do the math on that by the way, if the Indigo child phenomenon has been amplifying over the last 200 years particularly, but only 5% have made it to adulthood, then 'nature' itself is trying really hard to turn this tide. If you are 25 or over today, you are an exceptional soul and have made it through a gauntlet that most did not. Please hang in there! We need each and every one of us.

Those who do survive have developed keen survival tools. Many can successfully mimic five-sensed behaviour and harness their sixth sense successfully to take themselves to success in a specific field. Many successful sales people are six-sensed. Their additional sense allows them to hone in on an individual and sense what will make them comfortable, feel peaceful and make a purchase.

You'll find the six-sensed in focused fields too, somewhere where they can use specific focus to drown out the 'noise' of the world and their dedication is often noted and rewarded. Secretly they can also harness their sixth sense to help guide their work, but they will almost always cover 'inspiration' over with logical steps so they don't give themselves away.

Then of course we have the addicts. For me, Mate Gabor is the best source of information today on addiction and describes addiction perfectly as "seeking temporary relief" from the stresses and strains of life, but at a significant long-term cost. So if someone plays a game on their computer occasionally, seeking relief from their disturbing experience of life, that might be healthy and even helpful, but when someone spends more of their time in a game than in the world, and their life itself is negatively impacted, that would then be a harmful addiction.

Gabor also cites the origin of addiction as a lack of intimacy, the lack of human bonds – and that fits the Indigo Child perfectly, as they disconnect early from other humans whose inner moods and thoughts may differ hugely from their outward expression and that gives way to distrust of other humans. This then makes it difficult to form bonds with others, especially when we feel their inauthenticity or dishonesty.

So addicts are more often than not, six-sensed humans battling to live with the additional stream of information they've always received, but in their eyes, the rest of humanity denies, or demonises.

One addictive expression unique to the six-sensed is a peculiar cross-wiring of adrenaline and spiritual connection. The six-sensed that have shut off their connection with their true eternal spiritual selves will often reconnect in a time of crisis. When everything their human ego self has tried to control, manipulate or adjust goes haywire anyway, they finally surrender and in that moment of letting go, they reconnect, they re-open their communication with their Higher Self and life flows into wholeness all about them. Life is magical and for that moment, they step into their authentic selves and boy that feels good!

And life goes on and the crisis passes and all the old habits creep back in, the societal fears the hum-drum of grinding five-sensed 'reality' and the six-sensed cries out for the high of spiritual connection.
How did we get there last time?

Ahhhh – I remember, crisis!

And so the six-sensed pulls the pin on any little explosive devices they can find to recreate the crisis that drives them back to connection with spirit. The five-sensed might do this for the adrenaline rush but for the six-sensed, its pure energetic bliss to reconnect.

However that's really a long, arduous and painful way to get there. Just stop. Quiet your human mind, still the intellect, stop the churning, let go and soar into the truth of your real nature – you are a spiritual being having a human experience and your wings are always right there. You don't have to jump off tall buildings to force them open – you can simply surrender to their existence and allow them to open.

My favourite type of six-sensed human is what I call 'the porcupine'. Individuals with high emotional walls and often unwelcoming demeanours whose actions are just their way of keeping their distance from others. Their behaviour might be unconscious but you get the sense that there is a trigger at a certain proximity that the defences get thrown up, the crocodiles let out into the moat at the battlements are armed.

Through this method, they keep enough space about them to successfully manage the remaining information that comes flooding in. The problem with the porcupine is that they create in themselves a vast and insatiable hunger for human attachment and are likely to latch onto the first brave soul willing to brave the battlements and get over the walls.

The problem there being that not all adventurers who see a battlement and are inspired by the challenge of breaching it are good humans, worthy of deep emotional connection, and so this cycle will repeat over and over, painfully, causing only further reinforcement of the battlements.

Really, we are everywhere. Most of us hiding in plain sight.

I have a friend who is a very successful sales and marketing specialist. He's the perfect chameleon and blends into any global environment from Hallaal dinners in Dubai to rural village festivities in Africa. The man is awe-inspiring in his ability to adjust and blend into any setting, ensuring the comfort and receptivity of his clients. And authentically so, he doesn't fabricate empathy and alignment with those about him, he is a genuine chameleon who taps INTO his surroundings and becomes one with it. But the inauthenticity and dishonesty of corporate life wears on him to the point where at one stage he was working six months on and three months off – having to take breaks to recuperate from the wear of the fakery. His skills are greatly in demand so he would find a new placement with ease, just to be worn down by the same dishonest practices again and again.

He is clearly six-sensed and like many of us, he has learned how to excel in the five-sensed world, even when aspects of it repulse him. So even when six-sensed are successful in the 'normal' world, the toll on their overall state of being is a high one.

There are also the in-betweeners. These are historically five-sensed individuals whose sixth sense has either just activated or activated sometime in the recent past and they just don't really know what to do with it. Their habits of thought and behaviour are all five-sense anchored and so they live life as a five-sensed person, usually wrestling with their awakened sixth sense. These individuals can be confusing to encounter as they appear five-sensed completely, but you could feel an affinity with them that seems inexplicable. It takes a good deal of time – and usually a life-remodelling – for these individuals to align with living as a six-sensed human. So for the most part initially, I would think of them as 'five-sensed plus'.

Aligned with them are those of us who have learned to shut off our sixth sense as much as possible. We clamp down on the knowings, the seeing and the wisdom that flows to us either to fit in or because someone has made us think there is some 'ill' in what we are. But any promptings to harm any other, or the self, is not guidance from spirit, from the Higher Self, so there can be no harm to a six-sensed individual that stays focused light-ward and allows the guidance of their higher self to flow through them. These Indigo Adults who have shut down their inner guidance are often conflicted, unhappy and in enduring pain and only the encouragement of other Indigo's living productive and joyful lives might encourage them to reclaim their true selves.

So there is so much good to be done, simply in stepping into our authentic self and embracing our place in humanity's march towards a world of peace and harmony which must be the next step or the Indigo Children would not be being born in waves at this time.

What is it like to be one of us?

Depending on how successfully you've dampened your sixth sense, will determine the degree to which you'll relate to these statements:

You FEEL the life all around you. You can sit quietly and FEEL people everywhere. You may not have words for what they are experiencing, but you feel their joy, chaos or anger as clearly as if it were your own.

Humans make the most 'noise but you also feel other life, from the energy stored in crystals or the frequencies they hold to the striving of plants or the yearning of animals.

When you allow your intuition to guide you, you can have magical experiences of life flowing all about you, but when you doubt yourself and get mired in uncertainty, you can feel buffered and beaten down by the multitude of emotions that pass through you from everywhere.

When you do trust yourself and follow the promptings of your sixth sense, you see the synchronicity flow, you call the right person at the right time, end up at the right place at the right moment and life seems to wrap itself around you with gentle and loving guidance.

You cannot drive past and ignore injured animals or people. Their pain calls to you and there is no question in you that you will help whomever you can, whenever you can as you experience their needs as if they were your own.

You also know when there's something 'wrong' in someone, something 'off' that urges you to leave their presence immediately.

You try hard not to cause pain to others, even when it seems necessary, you know that the backlash of causing pain to them will hit you possibly more intensely than even they will feel it. Sometimes however, it will seem necessary, to protect another or to stand up for yourself and when you do, the impact of the hurt you cause – even for a good reason – may take you days or months to heal from.

You KNOW when you're being lied to, or when the person in front of you is not telling the whole truth. That doesn't mean you automatically know what the truth IS, but you know inauthenticity and dishonesty when you see it.

Humour defines a lot of us. The five-sensed will laugh uproariously at people falling over or tripping over something or humiliating themselves in some way. The six-sensed just experience the pain, humiliation or embarrassment WITH the person in the frame, even if they are 'just acting'. We cant understand what most people find funny or why. Often we will try to go along with the humour to blend in, but we don't understand it. Meanness of any kind, even if just pretended, offends us deeply.

Many of us hide pretty well in plain sight until we are involved in an incident that involves injustice, harm to an innocent or unjustified cruelty, and then – because we experience all of this WITH the victim, we roar.

Many six-sensed learnt early that a dedicated focus can help to drown out the 'noise' of the world and so most six-sensed are focused intensely on one area of life or another, in a specific career or field of interest. The five-sensed can misunderstand this to mean they are blinkered, that they have a one-track mind. But really, this focus helps them to stay sane. Because of this, they will protect this focus or protect their ability to focus on this area, almost to an unreasonable degree. But this is how they have learnt to survive in a world that makes no sense to them, outside of their area of focus.

We are usually more sensitive to materials – both those we wear and those we surround ourselves with. Natural materials like silk, linen, cotton or wool will uplift us significantly. If we surround ourselves with natural elements like flowing water, stone or plants, this too will help us maintain our equilibrium.

Until we learn to filter and tune our receptors, emotions can feel messy and chaotic to us as we're not only feeling our own but everyone else's. Emotion and six-sensed 'feeling' are the primary points of guidance for the human experience. When something feels right for us, it is, when something feels off or wrong, it probably is (or we're not lined up with it). So being either out of touch with our own emotions or feeling resistant to emotions in general because the world is full of so many that we can make no sense of, is a significant obstacle on the path of any six-sensed.

Digestion is the perfect example of how to handle incoming nutrients OR inputs and if the six-sensed handle incoming feelings or information along the same principles, they will be able to more fully harness their emotions and feelings.

So we chew on something for a bit (if its tolerable, if not, just spit it right out). We ingest, extract what we need and eliminate the rest.

Absolutely no point holding on to bits we don't need or serve no purpose!

For many years I used the image of helium balloons – I'd pick up a feeling, couldn't find anything in myself that could have given rise to that – so I'd tie it to a balloon and let it float away. Now I don't even need the balloon.

Before we learn to process the feelings we experience all day however, we can be emotional roller-coasters or seemingly stoic – ignoring all feelings on principle because they are TOO MUCH.

We don't do well with small-talk. Sure, we can learn to fake it, but the inanities couched in inauthenticity and noise wear on us. We'd much rather discuss something meaningful and life-altering.

There's an interesting correlation between the estimated percentages of 'Highly Sensitive People' and the estimation of those with an internal dialogue.
I was surprised to hear that some people don't have what studies have called an 'internal monologue' but further research would be needed to see if this could possibly be a six-sensed attribute representing real-time communication between the human and spirit selves.

By comparison: what is it like to live as a five-sensed human?

I cant know, I've never been one, but a client of mine that emerged into her sixth sense through meditation later in life explained it to me once.

In essence, it comes down to the adage that if you can't see it, hear it, smell taste or touch it, it doesn't exist. Everything that is exists in that narrow band of reality. You don't feel other people's emotions and many of yours you dismiss until they get loud enough. Action is at the heart of your day with DOING having much more importance than BEING.

If you were raised right, you'll do what you know is right, more out of a sense of duty than any personal investment. You don't know when you're stepping too far off your path – one thing can lead to another and you can find yourself in terrifying situations because you had no warning that you had gone wrong somewhere.

The dominant deterrent is fear, fear of embarrassment, fear of humiliation and fear of looking stupid or wrong.

I'm sure there's much more to it but for me, its enough to understand what we DON'T share with the five-sensed and so what elements of ourselves they will never understand.

My family adopts, people, animals and souls. We don't intend it, we don't go out looking to do it, but when God or Source puts someone or something in our path that we can be of assistance to, we do, as effortlessly as we would have our next meal or the next conversation. We don't find anything praiseworthy in our actions, the fact is there is never a choice. I've even caught myself feeling mild offence that anyone would think that we could NOT have done some of the things we've done. "Who would do that?" I ask myself, but then I have to remember, the five sensed would.

I'm not saying all six-sensed individuals come with saintly behaviour, we can be as resistant and personally conflicted as anyone, but we do because we cannot NOT do. In any safe environment we are kind by default, never mean and generous with our time and attention when needed.

Can you imagine the world we will one day demand to live in? When enough of us heal from the trauma of surviving to here, we could set a bar for the whole of humanity: A minimum standard of honesty, integrity and kindness.

Oh boy what a world that will be!

What is it about the five-sensed world that is so troublesome?

When the five-sensed encounter a lie, or they uncover a dishonesty, it's a three dimensional issue. Someone has told a fib. So be it. For the six-sensed, the feeling of dishonesty is visceral and impacts us to the core of our being.

Everything has a feel to it. Love is one that everyone knows, it feels lovely and warm and welcoming. Dishonesty too has a feeling, it feels sucking, clawing and oily.

In a simpler world, there were limited exchanges in a day, fewer exposures to possible lies, jealousies, envies or hatreds. Now the world is flooded with them, from advertising boards besides the road to our social media.

Because the information we are receiving is energetic, its a never-ending flow of ick and yuck and ewwwwww – until we learn to hone our focus to specific pleasing expressions.

But even as small children, the dishonesty of our parents or elders would affect us deeply, even if we would have to try to ignore our knowing in order to preserve those relationships. Trust would be eroded anyway.

The result was being bonded to people we didn't trust and feeling unsafe in the world. With no trusted guides to help us navigate this stream of information, our self-confidence is minimal and we get stuck in survival.

Anyone who knows Maslow's Hierarchy of Needs diagram will know how human beings in general first strive to achieve physical shelter and sufficiency, then safety. Love and belonging are next on the list of priorities and then status and esteem before we finally emerge into self-actualisation, a whole being whose very presence is of service to the world.

The six-sensed make a mess of Maslow's theories. Even if our physical needs are covered by our parents as a child, the chaos of adults' messy emotional states and lack of alignment with truth means few of us achieve a feeling of safety. Even if we fake that or develop tools to cope with feeling unsafe, unless we have at least one other six-sensed adult in our environment belonging is never achievable while surrounded by five-sensed others and bonding comes with all sorts of unique challenges that no-one stands ready to help us with. We know when people are being dishonest, we know when people are even talking about us behind our backs. Even if we are not tuned in enough to grasp the details, we feel the discomfort of the moment and that just causes us to withdraw further and further.

There's a particular sort of wear that comes from a 'knowing' that directly contradicts what we are seeing or that no one else is acknowledging.

Let me give one example. Let's set the scene at a spiritual or religious event. The Indigo Child is amongst a small group of individuals who are gathered together to focus their attention on some kind of Good. Perhaps there is prayer or worship of some sort involved. One figure in the group is the focus of a lot of respect and admiration from the group, but the Indigo Child KNOWS, with every fibre of their being, that this individual who is being admired and venerated, oozes evil. Their intentions are selfish, their energy is 'ill' and their behaviour is disingenuous. But all the caregivers of this Indigo Child are admiring and respecting this individual too so the child mind is confused. Do they not see that this person is NOT GOOD? If they do, why are they sucking up to him? If they are my exemplars, then does that mean I have to bow down and grovel before evil? Confusion reigns – not only on what to do about this ill individual, but how now to trust our care-givers.

The easiest resolution is to accept that there is something wrong with us, that we are the problem – but self-distrust at such an important developmental age can have significant impact later on. What we really learnt in those situations was that it was alright to deceive others, be inauthentic and ego-driven, but living in that way will destroy the six-sensed from the inside out. It is one thing to pick up on every feeling that is thrown around, and be uplifted by some, but in this society, repulsed by most. It is quite another thing when the repulsion is at your own self. When YOU become the source of the dishonesty, the inauthenticity and the injustice, there is nowhere to go to get away from what is within you.

The Indigo Children remember are those six-sensed BORN, so are assaulted with this additional stream of information from the first moment of their birth, so when reasoning and mature understanding is not yet in place, they are still receiving ALL this information. In a five-sensed world, a lie is only a lie when its proven. In the world of the six-sensed, a lie sounds like a musical key that is flat or dull. It has a recognisable resonance to it and you KNOW it when you hear it. What you don't know and cant understand is why everyone around you is believing it. Young life for an indigo child is a particular kind of hell.

Sadly, genuine psychopaths and narcissists are some of the easiest people for us to be around. They are remarkably 'quiet'. Their energy seldom feels messy and they don't feel as unstable and wounded as most other humans. This will always end badly, but they are unique in their attractiveness as their energy feels clearer and cleaner. These personality types don't hold the potential for a deep, healthy emotional bond and the six-sensed are frequently damaged by them, but at first they present a refreshing change from most people whose inner chaos is as obvious to us as storms in the sky.

We crave intimacy with others, but our self-isolation lends us to overcompensate when someone breaches the walls and we over-bond – sending them running for the hills or causing us both pain.

If we do manage a healthy connection, our insightfulness will often frighten five-sensed partners away so belonging too is a field of thorns.

Self-actualisation, for the six-sensed, is best achieved through the spiritual leap over the other stages and directly into a relationship with Source, God, the Divine or as some people call it, the Universe – for its there that we at last find a connection that is kind, supportive and loving and unfailing. Spiritual practice of some kind gives us a form to follow, helps us to self-manage and the others in that same practice open up opportunities for belonging.

There can be many intellectual hurdles to finding the spiritual practice that's right for you, of course one that doesn't demonise any six-sensed expression would be best, but even there, there are pit-falls.

Prayer and meditation with both amplify the sixth sense, so praying in a room with a group of others can be profoundly disturbing when they are secretly harbouring resentments, prejudices and animosities that are clearly visible to any six-sensed individual present. Only with supreme detachment from the thoughts and opinions of others can a six-sensed individual be comfortable in spiritual practice with a room full of five-sensed others. We will find their dishonesty and inauthenticity repulsive in such a setting and often be deeply injured by the seeming injustice of finding ugliness in what we hope will be a bliss-filled setting.

Making anyone aware of our deeper insight is seldom helpful as it sets off chains of fear and personal animosities, making those environments uncomfortable to return to.

In a five-sensed setting, what is clear to us – if not accompanied by photographs or 'hard evidence' – is irrelevant anyway and easily denied by individuals who don't share a strong sense of truth.

Their hollow flowery words will disturb us – not from a place of judgement, we are not in any way proclaiming ourselves to be the judge of others – we FEEL the hollowness, the inauthenticity and the way it FEELS disturbs us. No, we don't have evidence that this or that person is being inauthentic, we don't need evidence to EXPERIENCE the inauthenticity of a behaviour or attitude, we just know it when we encounter it. Sorry.

But still, a spiritual practice, can help us transcend the rungs of Maslow's personal development model, especially if we remain compassionate to the limitation of the five-sensed and remain aware that our vision in most instances wont be shared with many.

The ideal of course would be a spiritual environment that guides all their members to pray and meditate daily, perform some sort of self-assessment everyday and where individuals are left to create their own relationship with their Higher Power – not subject to the judgement or egos of others. If the members of such a group actually followed that guidance, they would all become six-sensed and then we'd be exploring a whole other topic: How to help the five-sensed adjust to life as a six-sensed human. Hopefully that future is not too far away.

For now, peace in those environments comes from knowing that you really are possibly the only person in the group who sees that Mabel is in pain but hiding it well, that Mark is overwhelmed but keeping a stiff upper lip and to stay well clear of Amos because he's a hot toxic mess of internal chaos. Be aware of who in your environment is five-sensed and who is possibly six-sensed and understand that these are two separate breeds of humans (for now). It is unlikely that any five-sensed individual will ever understand or see you and you are unlikely to understand them. If you can make peace with that, you can control your expectations of others and minimise the pains of disappointment and misunderstanding.

A whole world in which the six-sensed would be a peace is one where honesty would be the minimum standard and nothing less than kindness would be tolerated. In the ideal world of the six-sensed, each individuals own path of growth would be respected, and there would be no judgement of others' choices. Of course doing no harm would be in there too but if your bliss was to live in a hut in the jungle, there would be no judgement of that, in fact all your friends would celebrate your alignment with your purpose and wish you all the best – and MEAN IT!

There would be no poverty or human cruelty since just the thought of either of these things is painful to us. There would always be someone to reach out to to share a tea and a few thoughts with – to 'consult' on any issue you were challenged by.

There would be a system of governance for sure, but without parties and politics and lies. People would just vote for councils of people that they believed would be good administrators of public affairs, secretly and with no self-promotion.

Affairs would be governed locally, cultures respected and neighbours would all look out for each other.

This is not paradise for a six-sensed human, this would be the MINIMUM standard of life that we would find tolerable.

Democracy itself is a fine concept, but it almost doesn't translate into anything meaningful in the world without the six-sensed.

Humanity has been too easily fooled by agendas. The 'ruling class' still exists today and has socially engineered the globe towards its most profitable and ideal environment – for its own good. But it could only do so through lies, half-truths and manipulations of truth.

There may no longer be Monarchies in most regions of the world, but those who rule now are the owners of all the 'things'. A little research would show anyone who those people are – perhaps 500 or so individuals but with legacies that go back centuries. They have been at this for a while.

Just as 'nature' and the prompting of Spirit have been at the awakening of the sixth sense of mankind for a while.

The second of these two sets of momentum, the natural momentum of mankind to 'better', not just for a few but for all, will proceed regardless, it is a law of nature to improve, to grow and to evolve. It is the first set of people who have tried to oppose this natural evolution and bend it to their own will.

Where did it all go wrong?

If you accept the idea of Eudaemonic Resonance – the principle that life will lead you forward to natural self-growth and happiness if you follow what feels better in yourself, like a plant reaches for light and warmth or an animal tends towards belonging to a group – then how did this all go so wrong for mankind? How did we start bucking the flow of life to move away from 'better' to worse and worse? And here I'm not just referring to the six-sensed, we went along for the ride for sure but it is really clear that at some point mankind went from a curve of steady growth and evolution to enslavement to false systems and autocratic rule.

Once people became aware of the social engineering that was being employed to manipulate humanity, a few experts emerged in various fields that could predict happenings based on the nature of the propaganda that was being promoted at the time. Its not a difficult thing to become aware of – what are people trying to convince us all is best for us and the world? Does that make sense to you? It's usually happening to try to hide something or manipulate a set of people. It's simple to spot when you understand the basic principles.

So while people will generally trend towards what feels better, so love, harmony, unity and understanding, you can see through history a set of influences that run counter to that. Behind all inspired conflicts or attempts to pit one people against another, is greed.

A French Foreign Legion Agent said that to me once and it took me years of deliberation and research to understand what he meant – but when you see it, it cant be unseen. Running right through history is a quest for resources and the manipulation of societies or specific groups within societies to motivate annexing those resources. War or open conflict is about resources. Every. Single. Time.

The structure of present day society is no different. Most of the struggles and pains we endure are from fake, imposed structures that we don't question because they are presented as 'the way things are', but to the six-sensed, the very structure of society feels wrong. The financial services industry feels wrong – because it really is for the most part morally reprehensible. Most corporations are run by psychopaths within oppressive regimes that celebrate all the wrong kinds of things. And so the challenges to the Indigo Child do not end with graduating high school. Then they are launched into a society out of balance, immorally structured and oppressively run.

I'll encapsulate that for you in a picture that struck me the other day. There was an elderly gentleman walking across a car-park. He was not wealthy at all, he likely survived on a meagre pension. He held in his hand a plastic bag from a chain-store containing a few items and a clear plastic bag containing a loaf of bread. In the other hand he was drinking a well-known fizzy drink that I would never want anyone I cared about to put in their bodies because its full of refined cane sugar and chemicals. But there he was, probably on his way home from purchasing a few simple things.

I worked with elements of the financial services industry for many years so I know that field quite well. In that one transaction, any of us can know that first, the banks made some money there – a transaction fee for the purchase or from receiving and paying out whatever funds he had. Even if he paid for those goods in cash, the banks will make money on receiving that cash so the banks benefited regardless. The drink he was drinking costs almost nothing to make from chemicals and processing so there was a profit on that drink of at least 75%, in which the chain store shared, and the other small items in his packet too would have made a profit for the store.

Interestingly, if you track the owners / shareholders of that chain-store and that bank, you will today find the same group of people. And those people are already wealthy beyond words. So on the one hand there is a gentleman, in his sunset years, scraping by, and everything he does, every purchase he makes like this one, makes some set of very wealthy people in the world, wealthier.

I'm not anti-business or making money, but there's something wrong with this picture. I FEEL it, before I can put words to why – I can FEEL the wrongness of it, and this is what the six-sensed are assaulted by every moment of everyday out there in the world.

If the same picture included a lady baking bread at home and selling it directly to customers, perhaps with a fruit-juice she made from fruit she grew in her garden, it would feel much better.

Are you seeing it yet? There is nothing wrong with YOU. The world feels wrong because it IS wrong – for you. Five-sensed individuals can happily survive in a world where there are people starving just next door. It might disturb them intellectually a little, they might even think it sad, but it doesn't cause them any real unavoidable pain. They don't have to go through life with blinkers on praying they wont come face-to-face with an injustice or an unkindness today, because it wouldn't bother them too much if they did.

You and I creep gently through the world dashing from here to there trying not to be overwhelmed by all the wrongness that is everywhere.

And that is why most of us don't survive, but its also why the world is not already healed, whole and a blissful place to be. But we didn't fail to heal the world on our own as Mrs Tappe hoped we would, besides all the challenges of being six-sensed humans in a five-sensed world, we've had significant opposition.

Alyce Dylan

The 'ruling class' as I've referred to before – some of whom were once monarchies and then stepped back into the shadows with a group of very wealthy 'elites' have been actively working against the evolution of mankind into six-sensed reality and their version of the future is terrifying. This is no longer theory, it's a provable fact that experts have dedicated much time to tracking through recent time.

During World War II, the Nazi scientists did a lot of research on six-sensed individuals. It was them that first discovered that fluoride, that has absolutely no health value, calcifies the pineal gland and therefore dulls the receptor of the sixth sense. After this war seemed to end, this chemical was added to the waters of the world – everywhere.

There is an abundance of research and truth dossiers available on just this one topic if you do some objective independent research to show you clearly, that 'the powers that be' are not fans of those with six instead of five senses. Fluoride is a waste-product from aluminium manufacturing. Its waste. The only thing fluoride is 100% proven to do is calcify the pineal gland, the part of the body that has the highest frequency and is therefore believed to be the receptor for the sixth sense.

The Nazi's figured that out. They documented it. A few years later, the worlds municipal water supplies were flooded with it. This is not rocket science. I urge you to do this research for yourself and try to assign any other conclusion to why this step was taken globally, within decades of the end of that war. And who is it that had that reach? Who could have implemented that plan globally? What for?

The conclusion I have to go with is that it does not serve the 'ruling class' – or some element of it anyway, for there to be a segment of society that can instinctively tell truth from lies and feel the wrongness of something – even if they don't claim to know what the 'right' way would be.

So if you've always felt somewhere in your being that people were out to get you, there may just be a glimmer of truth that would result in that translation – there really have been a whole lot of people who worked hard at trying to PREVENT you from being, and for those who made it through *that*, to make sure you were assigned to the fringes of society where your voice could not be heard and would not be credible if it was.

It might be a comforting thing to know, it gives us reassurance that the sense we have of persecution isn't entirely unjustified, but its also irrelevant to what comes next. If in nature, there was a great big body of water reaching to join with the sea, some beaver-types could dam it up for a time, they could divert it somewhat – but eventually it WILL reach its goal. We are that river, and eons of momentum of the evolution of mankind are behind us – and when we reconnect to Source and find our guidance, we are empowered beyond anything that can be set against us. So you can acknowledge the opposition, you can see it stretching back through history, you can see the manipulation today – and then let it all go.

The most important step for the six-sensed to take today is to heal, to achieve wholeness, and, harnessing the wonder that comes with this additional sense once it is embraced, set new standards for humanity through our own choices.

More?

Here are some additional perspectives that can make it easier for a six-sensed individual to thrive in the world today:

An interesting question to chew on, like one of those debate-starters at dinner parties that add an additional course as 'food for thought':

If human sight can see 10% of the real spectrum of light that surrounds us, given the opportunity to expand that sight to say, 40%, would you take it?

The array of responses range from: "No way! Life is enough of a challenge with what I can already see, why take on more?" to, "of COURSE, who wouldn't want to see what's really all around us?"

Well what if you had been born with 40% light perception in a world where everyone else was only taking in 10%?

That's a good analogy to use to explain to a five-sensed what it is to be born with six senses.

From the experience of other six-sensed individuals we can build a broad picture, and I promise I've never heard of any individual whose sixth sense activated that ran away screaming in horror. So whatever Hollywood has tried to frighten us with, the reality is far gentler and more nurturing than any fears that might come up.

Many spiritual paths already contain the advice to entertain practices that WILL awaken the sixth sense anyway, meditation, yoga, even heartfelt prayer are some of these. You could say that along spiritual paths that recommend or require those practices, the followers should all by now BE six-sensed, but the call of material reality and limiting historical train of thought can be tough to let go of, so the theory is sound, even if the practical reality is less than what we could hope for.

Environmental and Energetic awareness

So the first thing the sixth sense gives us is greater awareness. We can pick up the energy of a room, the 'vibe' of a place or between people. We can more accurately assess peoples' state of being and can develop true empathy with other beings, human and other.

With the sixth sense being so newly applied to more than one or two members of a tribe, there is so little that we know about its possibilities and potentialities.

Many six-sensed get stuck in a lane. 'I'm a clairvoyant now, and that is different enough from everyone else out there that I'm going to stop there', is the feeling of those out there on the leading edge. And those individuals have so few peers to discuss their interpretations with and share their experiences with that they can go off on tangents that leave the realm of reason with no-one really to stop and kindly ask them, couldn't what you're receiving mean this, or that?

We will get there together, but for now the six-sensed who have made room for themselves in the world feel they are forging out alone and they do so bravely, but with little to guide them to stay relevant to the human experience.

Creation and spiritual awareness

The next world is truly 'within' this world, separated by a veil. The sixth sense allows us to penetrate that veil and communicate with souls on the other side. They are not 'dead people' as they are very much alive, but they once were in human manifestation and now are not.

There are no 'evil spirits' on the other side of that veil. The only 'evil' I've ever encountered through the use of my sixth sense were all of human origin. There can be dense emotions in a place that can make it feel 'wrong' or 'off', but those are usually residual energetic impressions left behind after a traumatic or tragic event. These spots get fed with human attention and can grow, or someone with the know-how can come along and clear the energy of that space.

So with the sixth sense, we can develop or naturally just have from birth, the ability to communicate with people who have passed on. But we don't need to, it is not a requirement nor would we ever be forced to if we chose not. A friend of mine that is six-sensed had one encounter ever of a relative that was in the next world and it disturbed her so much, that she asked (and prayed) never to be contacted again in such a way, and they never have.

Your supporters, ancestors, helpers and guides in the next world will never ask more of you than you are ready for or comfortable with and their purpose in making contact would only ever be to help, to serve you in some way or support your journey.

There may be lessons they did not learn while in human manifestation, and in walking with you through your experiences, they get to complete their incomplete learning. As you heal, you share healing with them too and so it is very much a mutually beneficial relationship.

You are, after all, a product of their lives and loves, and any damage they left unhealed will have carried down to you. I imagine it is their responsibility on the other side, to aid in the healing of any of the damage they introduced to their line, before they can move on, and so they will try to guide and support you in that healing, for you, but also for their own path.

The experience of those souls however is just loving, great vistas of love and care. Having experienced that with every person I've ever met, I wonder that anyone ever feels 'alone'. There is such love, care and compassion coming at you in every moment from all your 'peeps' on the other side, that you are never, not for one moment, ever alone.

But of course if you have self-isolated, as a six-sensed human, to protect yourself from the noise and confusion of the world, then it is understandable that you feel that way, just so long as you understand it is never actually the case. The lower your vibration, the less likely you are to be able to feel the invisible support that is there for you – the higher your vibration, the easier it is to tune in to those who are now AT that higher vibration.

Your unseen soul-people stand ready and willing to help and support your process in any way they can, you just need to ask.

The other kinds of spirits that you can become aware of is the world around you.

If you think for a moment of the complexity of the human experience, of the subconscious mastery of breath and growth, healing and manifestation that we must have already come with into this human experience, you surely must consider that we existed before we got here to this human experience.

Prior existence must have prepared us for this human manifestation in some way and with the sheer volume of complexity of human existence, it could possibly have been a very long journey indeed.

In a Course in Miracles, there is an explanation of our origin as spiritual beings that has always felt closer to the truth than any other image I've encountered. There they paint the picture that we are sparks, flying off the bonfire at the centre of the Universe (the bonfire being the Creator), flinging ourselves off to the outer edge of Reality to be a part of the Expansion of Reality, and that far from the blaze of the Creator, to experience our own light. This light is a reflection of the Creator anyway, but we get to nurture and grow our little spark through our journey.

That analogy makes a certain logical sense to me. Put that alongside Abraham Hick's assertion that we come to this reality to become co-creators in the process of Expansion, and a possible scenario emerges.

As sparks of the central blaze of the creator, if we fling ourselves out to the edge of Light, in order to shine ourselves, and to practice co-creation ourselves, and slowly make our way back to the centre of creation with all we have learned and experienced, and in that way expand the Collective Consciousness. Then this human reality is just one tiny fraction of our eternal journey.

As an extension of that idea then, we would start our practice of co-creation at the beginning. With the easy stuff, and move onwards from there.

The STUFF of the universe is not stuff, it is energy and frequency. Quantum Physics now tells us that all stuff is indeed energy. So what you're sitting on there, energy. What you ate earlier – also energy and that cup of coffee? Energy too.

Quantum Physics tells us that all matter is just energy, vibrating at different frequencies. All of what we think of as 'stuff' is really at its core non-stuff, the frequency of which has slowed down enough to manifest into the world of BEing AS stuff. But the stuff is the result, not the beginning.

So in order to 'make matter', as spirit-beings, it stands to reason that we would need to learn to slow the frequency of energy right down and maintain it at a certain frequency, perhaps for a really long time. That sounds rather like the Mineral realm to me.

Imagine, there we are, floating about as spirit, and we enter level one, slow down some energy to make one particle of stone. Practice long enough and perhaps we get to make really special stones, crystals, diamonds etc. As a step in the practice of co-creation, that would be some great victory.

And once we had mastered all the skills needed for solid, enduring matter, perhaps we move on to the Vegetable Kingdom and spend a few eons participating in microbe and then algae manifestation, perhaps lichen, then grasses, flowers and even trees. We learn the process of photosynthesis, absorption and reaching for light. I imagine we fail more than we succeed but we grow and learn and get better and better until, when we are ready, we pop into the Animal Kingdom.

Insects first, in groups perhaps, then going off alone as solitary beings. We're building momentum now after a long time learning the very basics so lives here are maybe shorter, fireflies, crickets and other living beings. Learning the skills of movement on top of digestion and transmutation. As birds we experience flight, as fish we adventure in the deep. Advanced beings I imagine would be elephants, dogs cats, monkeys, dolphins and whales – and there we start to grasp emotions overlaying instinct.

We can approach this idea from a different direction – have you ever watched a human child and marvelled at everything they already know? They already know SO MUCH by the time they are born into this human experience!

They know what to do with their hands, they know how to get attention, they understand so much more of their world than a being would that had just popped into creation, even beyond instinct.

And if you chew on that for a while and you can see a level of understanding in new-borns that doesn't logically tally with something that just began its existence today, then could you make room for the idea that the self that is now manifesting into human form, has perhaps been at the practice of manifesting for eons, through the mineral, vegetable and animal realms?

And what if, in that process of manifesting each time, you got to experience life AS those things? You would need to hold the focus and the intention OF the vibration OF that element to manifest it and so while you need not BECOME entirely that manifestation, your experience during the period of manifesting into the world AS that thing would be the experience of the life you were manifesting. And as you worked through progressively more challenging manifestations, you would acquire the virtues, the skills and faculties of that form of life. Minerals perhaps just holding solid form, as plants through growth and synthesis, insects and animals would teach everything from growth to movement and emotion.

This perspective can also explain why we have such affinity for certain animals or plants or even stones – because they WERE once a part of our journey to here.

With so many lives behind us, having mastered all forms of manifestation, we might finally be ready for Human Manifestation, where we acquire true consciousness, and here we acquire a Soul. We were always spirit, our manifested forms were the vehicles through manifested experience, and the Soul will be our vehicle into the next vistas of experience.

If we went through all of that to get HERE, then just Being here is a victory, a tremendous achievement and a unique opportunity.

And in this human experience, through our sixth sense, we can also recognise the spirits of all created things, and learn to communicate with them. If this theory is correct, then behind each manifested being, there is a spirit that is co-creating that manifested reality, and through the language of energy, we can communicate with each and every one of those spirits.

Some people have fallen into that skill accidentally, without a picture of this possible reality, and find themselves naturally able to communicate with various species. Our only hurdle to being able to do this, is our perception of reality.

Can you see the possible implications of the knowledge that all of this earth's manifested reality, all the organic substance of this world, is all potentially humanity? On its way towards humanity? And what does that then make US, in our shining victory of co-creation? We made it, to HERE! The respect for and honour of all natural life that this makes room for can encourage us to offer greater levels of understanding and grace to all the elements of our surroundings and creates the foundation of a far greater, more unified and cohesive human experience.

This perspective is not mine. It is one laid out across many spiritual texts and religious writings, it has simply been misunderstood or overlooked within the grid of how we 'thought' then – that stuff comes first and gives rise to matters of spirit. But really, the opposite is true.

The next time you greet an animal or even a plant, try to see beyond the manifested being, to the spirit that is manifesting it. You will feel the connection. A true meeting of equals, separated only by time and experience.

This understanding of the world can explain so many misunderstandings incorporated into many 'esoteric' belief systems as spirits, having a human experience have tried to assign reason or meaning to feelings.

The path to joy and happy

"So does standard Psychology even apply to us?" - is one question I have been asked. And to some extent of course it must, we are human beings too and also struggle with ego and intellectually grapple with issues – but this field as it currently exists was for the most part created by five-sensed individuals, for the five-sensed and like many branches of Western Medicine has often been harnessed as a weapon AGAINST the six-sensed.

There ARE notable experts in this field that are clearly six-sensed themselves, and while their tertiary education seeks to box them into a zone of ideas, you can feel and hear from them the expansion of standard practice out beyond the rigid paradigms they have been indoctrinated with.

That is to say that in the field of mental health, the practitioners that could be of any benefit to the six-sensed are themselves operating outside of the strict application of their education. If a psychologist or psychiatrist is felt to be needed, just be very clear about finding the right practitioner for you, who is six-sensed too.

Most six-sensed already feel their isolation from the rest of humanity. They know they are not 'like them', so they tend to steer clear of programmes and self-help manuals designed for the public. Honestly a lot of it doesn't hit the mark and is clearly aimed at the five-sensed. But there are exceptions. A lot of six-sensed individuals are now in the personal growth and development arena (some just as authors) from Esther Hicks to Richard Bach and Jeff Brown, and can offer meaningful insight and guidance. I've always relied upon my sixth sense to guide me to my next steps in this area, what next book to read or what field to explore, and when you do that, the journey is a grand adventure as the next piece of the puzzle shows up, especially for you, and perfectly on time.

For humanity in general, being happy is now a popular field of study which is a good sign, signifying that a clear majority have had enough of all the struggle and strife of this skewed social paradigm and are looking to move on to higher vibrational states of being.

The art of being happy is said to be cemented in managing what we want and what we 'should' want is still being hurled at us relentlessly by a five-sense grounded world. Primarily we are told that we should want money, power and pleasure. These wants are temporary and might deliver some temporary enjoyment but are ultimately empty for five or six sensed lives.

The desires that are supposed to be more enduring are listed as faith, family, friendship and rewarding work in the path of purpose that serves the world in some way.

Let's look at that from a 6-sensed perspective:

Faith:

Because of some of the scenarios outlined before – faith is a difficult area for the six-sensed. Many lose or abandon their religious path early, not necessarily because of the teaching of that faith but the hypocrisy and inauthenticity they find in those environments. We all hold a higher standard for religious gatherings – whatever happens out in the world, in THIS space – be it at a church or a synagogue or a temple, we hold an expectation that HERE, people will be kind, honest and authentic.

And then we perform faith-based practices like prayer with this group of people that heightens our sixth sense and – eeewwwwwwww!

We can walk away from those gatherings feeling dirty, vomited on and sandpapered by everyone's secret thoughts and real intentions which to us are as clear as their pretty hats or fancy shoes.

It's only later in life, having survived our own struggles, hurdles and challenges that we can expose ourselves to all this blatant human chaos with compassion, but even then it's still unpleasant to immerse ourselves in the gatherings.

Faith as a personal journey however – absolutely! It's almost vital to finding balance and meaning. So if we investigate all the possible paths and find truth somewhere that calls to us and feels good and honest, that will be of great benefit on our path. But this is not the way it's usually done. Normally we go to an event and ask questions of a gathering – but this path to faith is more likely to keep us AWAY from religious or spiritual paths.

It is a comforting lesson to learn to entirely separate a belief system from the people who follow it as no true assessment of a spiritual path can be done by looking at the followers.

I was raised across two systems of belief. The adults that I accompanied to the activities of the first system were beautiful souls. Honest, authentic and shining examples of truly GOOD people. But the belief system they subscribed to was limited in comparison to the system of belief of the second.

The second religious group made so much sense to me – even as a child. It still makes the most sense to me today, but the people that took me there were messy, and I still struggle to attend any kind of large gathering – even with compassion and detachment.

I still subscribe to the second, it even encompasses most of the first – but I shrink from the participation in the gatherings of the followers. Since daily prayer and meditation are requirements of the practice, all the followers should be six-sensed after some short time, but individual choice is very much respected on this path and every person gets to create their own relationship to the Divine so most people don't and so it is a majority five-sensed environment. Individuals are often mean, inauthentic and inhospitable – and I am repulsed by their inner struggles projected outward.

By comparison, I was absorbed into a community of alternative healers when I began my journey towards Reiki Mastery some decades ago and by comparison, I was in awe of the kindness, gentleness and magical spirit of this group of people. I LOVED their company and found so many individuals in that group I actually WANTED to spend time with.

I came to understand however that they were the most disorganised and fragmented group of people. They were a balm to my soul and a delight to my spirit, and if they ran the world nothing would work.

I was at a crossroads, the religious group I was an active member in was a perfect fit in terms of tenets and ideals, but some of the people were repulsive- to my six-sensed self.

(I have to make the note here that groups of people anywhere, in a mall or at any gathering will almost always have a few people that a 6-sensed would find repulsive, so this is not a reflection of this or any group specifically, throw collective prayer into the mix and its just amplified). The healing community on the other hand was loving, kind and delightful company, but completely impractical and had some very bizarre theories on life, the universe and everything.

The juxtaposition created a crisis of faith for me as I was still striving to 'find my tribe' in the world as a six-sensed human trying to navigate five-sensed existence. I meditated on the issue, prayed on it and searched for an answer to where I belonged?

Within a few short months I was invited to serve the International body of my religious group for nine days. I would be flown to the Administrative Center and meet with the globally elected body to see if I could be of service to them in an area I was specialised in.

And when I did get to meet with five of the nine global representatives (democratically elected from across the world), I found the answer to my months of questioning. THEY were kind, gentle and authentic and beautiful souls, just like those of the healing community. But they were also rational, reasoning people, who followed earnestly the teachings I've always felt aligned to. I knew then that the path I followed was either capable of attracting individuals that were six-sensed, or it made them so and that there was therefore room for me, as a six-sensed individual within that group. Just perhaps not in the day-to-day gatherings.

You may find other six-sensed individuals in spiritually focused collectives, and have the opportunity to form deep and delightful bonds with them or at least have fantastic and meaningful conversations - so its well worth exploring this avenue, as long as you manage your expectations of others based on the understanding that five-sensed individuals may never achieve the levels of kindness, authenticity and honesty you will expect from a God or Good-focused community, but they will at least be making the effort.

Gatherings of five-sensed individuals however will always be wearing and chaotic unless you harness some pretty effective tools to get through them (I do go into some of those tools in a bit), so for the most part, the six-sensed will stay at home with their fur-friends or curl up with a book.

And then there is the argument that the focus in finding a path for you, cant all be about you. That the importance of participating in a collective is as much about what you bring to that collective as it is about what you get out of it.

And yet, that is a problem. This body of followers I spoke about before is a pure democracy – so reflects the way we would like the world to work, that we all have a say and a level of participation in the communities in which we live. This dilemma then is the perfect example that demonstrates the challenge of the six-sensed and their environment today.

We shrink from unkindness, ugliness and inauthenticity and so we self-isolate and our emotional survival depends on being really selective about what we expose ourselves to. Its really not about being selfish, in the sense that we DON'T care about anyone outside of ourselves, its about making sure that what we expose ourselves to doesn't leave us in a quivering mess on the floor.

But that also removes our voice from the collective – which then remains five-sensed driven and our resulting communities remain anchored in five-sensed ideals and imperatives.

Without our voice, our world will never be the kind, nurturing home that we all know it could be – but for that to happen, we need to be whole, healed and participating – 'out there' where we can both demonstrate and emphasise through our own example a new minimum standard for humanity: Be Kind. Be humble. Be honest and authentic. Be at peace with all other beings.

Family:

But I digress, I was examining happiness and the six-sensed individual. Next on the list is family – and that is another can of worms for the six-sensed.

Our parents probably exposed their dishonesty and authenticity to us long before we had the emotional maturity to buffer that disclosure and so if we have any lasting relationships with our parents it will be because we have done a lot of healing work or they were six-sensed themselves or exceptional individuals. For the most part, the six-sensed come from traumatic childhoods (mostly due to the information received from their sixth sense) and forming families of their own is a challenge. Not having a happy experiential blueprint to work from means we often don't have any experience of the kind of family we would like so there's a journey here of piecing together from experience what we do and don't want.

There is hope, I have known couples who were either both six-sensed or one of each five and six sensed that have worked very well. In the latter, the five-sensed is very tolerant of and initially amused by the 'eccentricities' of the six-sensed partner but often later will come to see their six-sensed partner as authentically 'gifted'.

If two six-sensed individuals are open to forging new territory and have a shared spiritual belief system, beautiful things are possible.

Carl Jung also proposes that we "recreate the relationships with or between our parents in order to heal them" and I've found this to be true of all the individuals I know or have worked with on their healing journey. We also attract what we are comfortable with, not necessarily what is good for us.

Those two tendencies together can mean that we manifest relationships with five-sensed individuals that are critical of our extra perception (if our parents were) or with people who will never understand us. In standard psychology, its an additional cog in an already complex wheel.

In my experience, six-sensed individuals tend see the potential of things, people and even businesses by default. This can be a marvellous talent, until the person you see as a majestic warrior princess reveals herself as a resentful and angry harridan in her present reality. This one takes a great deal of acceptance to navigate so lets begin by emphasising what value we contribute to the world with our default focus of attention on the best in situations, people or enterprises. What we 'pay attention to' is reinforced and supported and so all the potential and wonder we see in the world will in fact support the realisation of what we see.

However – and its a big one – we really do need to give all these things and people time, to show us their current truth – while still allowing our focus to remain on the glorious potential of all of it.

People tell us that we wear 'rose-tinted' glasses or some like adage and I say, "Yes I do! The world looks much better this way." And yet we need to make room for whatever we are seeing to – in present day reality – be possibly a fraction of what we 'see'.

Remember, its all about frequency and this I believe is one of the natural orders ways of making the world more habitable for us. Things (and people most of the time), just look better to us, we see their love and their yearning and their magnificent potential shinning out of them like a beacon; and the reality of all of that can feel like a whack in the face with a wet fish if we don't leave room for whatever we are observings' present-day reality to be just possibly less than it could be.

It is a common realisation for a six-sensed individual to come to that while they would like to spent eternity with the person THEY see when they look at a specific individual, but not a moment more with that person's present-day reality.

We navigate this pitfall with AWARENESS. Just know that life has given you this blessing of seeing and being able to pay attention to (and therefore feed and reinforce) the BEST of people, places or enterprises but if you want to bond yourself to any of these, you may need to dig deeper into the present-day reality of them.

In the world today the solid, mutually supportive, spiritually aligned relationships are the exceptions and not the rule – so happiness there is going to take perhaps more work for the six-sensed than the normals if we're going to try to find happiness through our own family.

Alyce Dylan

Work and Purpose

Work in a calling that is of service to the world is far more likely a source of happiness for the six-sensed. It provides a point of focus to drown out the chaos of 'out there', the resulting good feelings provide inestimable reward for the six-sensed and when they are working in some area of interest to them, they are likely to be very good at what they do. Afterall, they have an exceptional advantage over any five-sensed in their field through their intuitive faculties.

So you will find happy six-sensed individuals in a work environment where they can be specialised in specific areas and be very good at what they do. But as whole human experience this kind of life is incomplete, unbalanced.

The primary hurdle to the six-sensed finding true happiness is their own authenticity. Carl Jung said that people find happiness by acting according to their own principles.

So we find or evolve a set of principles as human beings and if we act in accordance with those principles, we should be happy.

Here's the problem: In order to survive in the five-sensed world, we, the six-sensed have had to hide or deny most of who we are. We have had to adopt modes of behaviour we don't agree with and participate in systems that feel wrong to us. And we've done all of this believing we had to because WE were the aberrant ones – or so we thought.

We may have come a long way down that road of not being our authentic selves and possibly have built whole lives on the foundation of a lie or at least a partial truth.

Had we adopted a set of principles based on our authentic natures, we would not tolerate any harm to anyone or anything and would not participate in any practices which caused harm. But we had to chop off those instincts and impulses just to survive in society and so we are, everyday, now acting against the principles we would have adopted had we known that our principles COULD be different from those around us because we were part of a new breed of human.

In essence, pretending to be 'normal' when we really are exceptional makes us morally inconsistent with ourselves, and that path will hold no happy until we clean up our authenticity.

So you can see why, according to Carl Jung, happiness could be elusive to the six-sensed human, based on these psychological parameters. HOWEVER, we can skip over all of that and simply tune into to happiness – that's possible – and life will respond by delivering to us happy happenings. We understand intimately the importance of frequency and energy, and when we step back from being assaulted by peoples frequencies and energies all the time and start to harness those frequencies – we can skip right to happy. On purpose.

A 'normal' person would say this is backwards, but we know the way they see the world is backwards. The five-sensed believe that everything starts with STUFF and that our experience of STUFF is the path to spiritual awareness. We KNOW that EVERYTHING FEELS like something, even STUFF and that it all breaks down to energy – so energy and frequency come first – and the STUFF is the result, not the beginning. Armed with this knowing, we have the power to tune in and focus to specific energies and the associated STUFF will follow.

Doesn't it make sense that we would be best suited to harnessing the energies and frequencies all about us for our good and the good of the planet? We feel these things all day everyday, we experience them. We know when they change.

We can imagine our sixth sense as a large invisible satellite dish whose default is to receive every scrap of information floating about – and as children, that's what we do. But we can learn quickly and quite easily to adjust the direction of that flow to OUT rather than IN. This way, if we conjure a feeling, say peace, or contentment, we can learn to sit IN that feeling and beam it outwards, to the world.

It is a struggle for five-sensed humans who get into visualisation or any other form of working with the laws and principles of creation to get a handle on working with frequencies. For the six-sensed, it's second nature.

And so here's the giant compensator. Life might have been a slog to here, Its possibly been a whole bed of very thorny roses – but NOW, if you can accept your true nature and harness the skills you already have in you but possibly have not yet explored – you can create a wonderful, fun-filled and meaningful life. Because YOU know how things FEEL, and if you can create the feeling, the things will fall into place to real-ise those feelings. Ha!

Yes I said it. The abilities that you may have felt have been more of a curse than a blessing are the same skills that will make you an expert tuner and amplifier of all the GOOD STUFF that this life has to offer. It just takes a little shift in perspective and some basic tools to begin.

Interpretation pitfalls & navigation

Standing here, on the edge of this emergence of a new breed of humans, we have to acknowledge how much we don't know. Yes, we are (and for Indigo Children, have been since birth) receiving an additional stream of information that most other humans don't seem to be aware of. But just as if we woke up one day in a foreign country where everyone spoke a different language, we might be receiving information but that doesn't mean we know how to accurately translate it yet.

For many of us, that additional information gets translated into the grid of understanding that we currently hold – so beliefs, fears and open injuries can colour the information we receive and skew it to fit those beliefs or fears.

Abraham Hicks is a collective who speaks through a medium called Ester Hicks. In one of her earlier interviews she explains how Abraham "chose" her to speak through because she was going to be a clear channel. She had almost no previous experience of anything esoteric and for the most part, held very few definite beliefs.

I have followed Abraham for years now and the only time anything said from that source ran in direct opposition to what I felt to be truth, was when Ester spoke from a place of a strong belief that she had previously held. Ester Hicks truly is a very clear medium, she seldom taints Abraham's message with ideas of her own but she has, and when she has everything about it felt wrong. To 'his' credit, Abraham always encourages everyone to tune in to their own inner knowing, so when these ripples have occurred, anyone tuned in could easily feel them as untruth – or as out of alignment. It's important to keep a balanced perspective therefore on any messages coming through others. Sometimes information comes in, and is interpreted and translated, and sometimes the information is coming from the individual's beliefs or understandings that is doing the translations.

The same is true for all of us, we will receive the information, but what we then make of it will be coloured by our own grid of preconceptions.

For this reason its important to start out working with our sixth sense for purely personal information. There are tools that can help to clarify the information – cards of various kinds and tricks like going to the bookshelf and opening a book to a line on a page, but nothing is clearer than simply receiving the information – even if we need to sit with it for a while and get ourselves out of the way of the information we are receiving.

Its due to the pitfalls of the translation of information, that we find ourselves with so many frankly odd and a little weird offshoots of communities that have attracted six-sensed individuals looking for a place of belonging.

It's always easier to walk a road with a friend or two than entirely on your own so the call of community is completely understandable. But with the sixth sense being so new to more than just a smattering of individuals, people's exposure to their own ability to receive and translate additional information so fresh (in terms of the history of the world), that a lot of strange fringe groups have emerged with some illogical ideas.

It is SO important that you hold fast to your own sense of truth. It's perfectly understandable how people skew so much innocent information into something self-aggrandising, but truth still needs to be YOUR compass. No one can plot your path to truth for you, its a road you need to walk and feel your way to.

Objective, unfettered independent investigation of truth is vital – and we have a backup system. We can read about a subject, see what is being 'said' out there, but we can also FEEL how that information feels to us.

Ask for truth and it will unfold like a flower before you. I kid you not, if you sincerely ask the Universe to show you truth, it will show up and you will KNOW IT when you encounter it.

Sometimes there is a grain of truth, encased in a lot of nonsense, but if you feel for clarity, you can sift out the elements of truth from what is being wound around it.

Alone in a sea of normal

I was fortunate in my childhood to have developed a form of ADHD, not the attention kind but the attachment kind. Compounded by my six-sense-influenced general withdrawal from others, the opinions of others meant less and less to me as I got older. What I did come to rely on was my 'knowing'. I didn't intellectualise it, I just knew if someone was a good person or not, or if there was something about to unfold that I should be wary of.

Into adulthood I trusted that knowing and it brought me much success in my own business efforts. Some might have called me 'excentric' because there were certain things I would not abide. Certain food chains I would never buy from, certain actors I could not stand to watch or certain products I would not support.

These were not beliefs I imposed on anyone else, they were just choices I made for myself but they were absolute. I could not even tell you why they were, but those things I refused to interact with just felt wrong and icky to me.

In recent years, justifications for 90% of those choices have emerged on the global stage with human DNA being found in certain foods, actors revealed as people who have made evil choices or products having been exposed as harmful in some way. I feel blessed that I had the temerity – sometimes despite a lot of peer-pressure – to stand my ground and simply choose, for myself, not to entertain anything that felt that wrong to me.

You won't always have the words for why or a reason that can be explained, just following your knowing will be enough. Some reasons will reveal themselves in time and some never will, but you will never go wrong following your inner guidance.

With the internet and all that's available there, its no longer information that is scarce but the means of sorting it out into worthy and 'not for me' that matters most.

With practice, even a newbie can feel what is true or not. This is something you can practice on your own. Say something true, then say something untrue. Feel for the difference. If you have a friend that can work with you, ask them to tell you true and untrue things alternatively and feel for the resonance of what IS true. For me, true things feel like a fresh spring morning – there's a crispness to truth that cant be replicated. Untruth on the other hand feels like the twang of hitting the bottom of a garbage can, it feels flat and hollow.

Skilful liars will wind an untruth around something true – and that can feel like a murky tapestry with one thread running through it. Sometimes someone with good intentions will grasp onto a thread of truth and run with it, encasing that truth with fluff and nonsense. So if you feel truth from something . . . but! - then you can delve deeper and find what IS true and discard the rest.

I love the idea that love means giving people enough room to fall down, but be willing to help them up. This life really is more of a rambling journey than an obstacle course – not everyone's end-point is the same. I've explored whole vistas of information that have called to me, only to discard 90% of it that didn't ring true to me and I've found that the 10 % I find here or there, always aligns with the truth I already resonate with.

In a five-sensed perspective, it would be argued that I'm selecting truth based on a framework I already hold, but new truths will often shake the foundations of my existing beliefs – and I am always willing to reassess. A new truth for me today however wont simply be an intellectual concept, it wont be a set of ideas, but a feeling and a resonance that tells me "there's something to look at here".

Sometimes that 'something to look at' will just be a door to a new vista that will take me closer to a truth, but I'm always glad I made the trip because the something I find adds to my broader understanding of how this all works.

The next set of information that calls to you might open you up to whole new vistas of exploration and while some of the information in this work might seem so new to you now, in a few years you might look back and think of this as 'rudimentary stuff'.

There are some 'esoteric' authors and speakers that feel like hollow vessels to me, but I can understand why the five-sensed might really benefit from their framing of certain topics; and then there are popular writers who frame themselves as six-sensed that I read and wonder what herbs they were smoking to offer such nonsense to the world. But I remain open to truth no matter what horse it rides in on, and so the threads of truth and the clarity they offer weave themselves together and strengthen daily.

A lot is dependent on what you are ready to receive. Sometimes even the clearest truths will only truly 'settle in' when you are truly ready to embody them.

On my Reiki Mastery Journey, I would often say to my Sensei – "Oh I know that", I guess then wanting to affirm my broader understanding of topics.

"Yes", she replied on one occasion, "you know that here" (pointing to my mind) "but you don't yet know it here" (gesturing to my solar plexus). "Sometimes, we need to let things live in our minds for a time before they fall into our BE-ing".

I have a picture now of those children's toys, the ones where a shape will fall through the hole of the same shape. Sometimes we can have the block, but we need to wait for the opening that *that* shape will fit through, for knowledge to be truly internalised. It's like a landing area for new information. We see it, it sparks for us. We acknowledge it, but only over time does it truly digest into our being – and then we are enriched, expanded and enhanced by that knowing.

You can often hear the resonance of someone speaking on a topic that is truly a part of their BE-ing. Wisdom that they not only think but that LIVES IN them can spread from them with clarity and depth that is visceral. When someone speaks on a topic they only think may be true, or that they are saying is true in that moment, the effect of their words will be shallow.

So we sift and sort through the incoming information, finding what resonates as true for us and perhaps chew on it for a while, digesting it through our existing grid and allowing it to make room for itself to inhabit our BE-ing. And once that process completes, we don't only know something intellectually, but energetically too. That truth becomes a part of who we then are everyday.

Your journey will be like that too. Your sixth sense will give you access to tremendous insight and constant guidance, but if we were meant to receive all truth at once, time wouldn't be necessary. We came into this human experience knowing it would unfold gently, that we would be able to piece things together and gather a whole picture of how this life really works and its okay that it doesn't reveal itself to us at once. Savour the truths you do find along your path and know that truth is its own self. Subjective truth is a myth and an evil one at that seeking to confuse the masses. Truth has a feeling, a resonance and an experience that comes with it that is unmistakable and if you are willing, it will unfold willingly before you. But like the saying goes, "first it might 'p' you off".

Real-isation

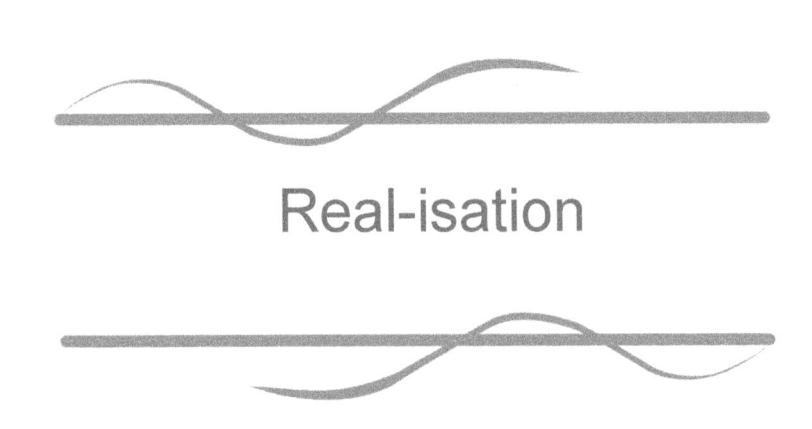

The perspective that really blew my mind when I first heard it, and still tickles me today – is the question of whether we are the originators of thought or the receivers of thought. I spent days analysing my thoughts asking of my faeries: "Was that mine or one of yours?"

If all is frequency and we are receiving all the time, then thought and feeling are the first stages of REAL-isation or translation of frequency or vibration into an 'earthly' vibration.

Did you come up with that thought or did you receive it?
See? Its a bit of a mind-pretzeler.

But if you do the maths, on how many people have lived, and are alive today, how many faeries there are beyond the veil of this life – just how many thoughts do you think COULD possibly be original?

After chewing on this for a while, I can feel the difference now, thoughts I have that are perhaps just manifestations of fears or worries – which then shows me what frequency I'm tuned into – and thoughts that are clearly not OF me – sometimes because I KNOW I did not have the grid of previous thought in place to arrive at that new thought.

The clearest way to frame this is that thought and feeling pathways are all translators of frequency – if that impulse comes from outside yourself, it could be inspiration. On the other hand if you are tuned to a lower frequency of doubt or fear, then you could be interpreting all the fears on that bandwidth. If these thoughts are not joyful, comfortable or at least interesting, you'll need to change the channel by tuning to a different band-width.

Appreciation is a wonderful tuner. Just look about you for all the things you can find which you appreciate: The sunny sky, the green grass, all the flowers and the trees getting on with being the best manifestations they can be. Appreciate it all, and in tuning to that frequency, more thoughts of things you appreciate will turn up effortlessly.

Making Contact

That same line in the book, A Course in Miracles, which describes the human spirit as having flown like a spark off the bonfire off the centre of the universe, or perhaps in another picture, dust off the robe of God, and is seeking to make its way back to re-union with that God or Source ties for me with the truth that we are all on a journey, called forward towards 'the light' and dancing each step of the way with shadows. Sometimes those shadows are of our own making when we 'get in our own way' and sometimes long shadows cast by others, up to no good. But there is no denying that the call towards union, re-union and intimacy with other souls is a clear one, for all of humanity.

If we see that call as an echo of the final goal – reunion with Source with all we have discovered and learnt along the way to add to the expansion of Source in some way, and understand that whatever we get to experience here will at most ever be an echo of the true union our spirit-selves desire, then we can more gracefully manage the expectation we hold of others.

We can share a journey for a time with this or that one, or even find our eternal match – but that it seems to me will be far more likely in the place beyond this world, which is so full of temptations and chaotic messaging. So we can find others with whom to share a part of the road. Perhaps some we might have shared history with, perhaps we manifested into the same wolf pack with them or buzzed it up in the same hive – and then there might be entirely new souls we get to experience for the first time.

For the six-sensed however, relationships are always going to be challenging in the present state of the world. What five-sensed human would want to be with anyone that can read their energy, know if they are being dishonest or just know they are really not as interested, even if they are pretending to be for some temporary pleasure or alternative motive?

There is not enough material available yet to write a book on relationships between six-sensed individuals, but I look forward to accumulating that (vicariously of course,; I only have one lifetime and am halfway through even that). How will it be to really see another person and be SEEN by them? How will it be to discover applications of the sixth sense together? I can imagine that will be a whole new vista of relating and intimacy, but first the Indigos especially will need to heal the wounds of surviving in a five-sensed world.

Along that road too it might be nice to have some fellow-travellers. So where do we find others like us?

We take a glimpse down that road of people on the 'alternative' fringe and we find a confusing mess of alien conspiracies and weird rituals and clearly unhinged individuals consistently high on ... something or other. And we go home and curl up with a book.

Yikes!
Not helpful.

"I know I'm different but ... Wow!"

And so the status quo remains, Indigo's and newly emerged six-ers self-isolating, as much from the five-sensed as from the six-sensed who have gotten carried away on some magical mystery tour – possibly with mushrooms and other greenery. And I say that with the greatest compassion and lack of judgement of anyone's path. It doesn't matter where you find the truths that make you a better human being, as long as they do no harm – but the alienating of the six-sensed has caused this series of spin-off detours that rational thinkers shrink from because it all seems too weird.

So we return to the question of wearing caftans and burning incense and if you have to take up playing a weird foreign instrument to live fully as a six-sensed human being and of course not!

Not unless you really really want to.

(and the caftans are made of silk :-)).

So what is a six-sensed human to do? If we DO get it, that we are a member of a new breed of human, and we do understand that the expectations we have held of others and society in the past that lead to such disappointment was based on not understanding all of this – what can we do NOW? Where do we go from here?

I've held gatherings of the six-sensed at my home sporadically for years now and the organisation of this has its challenges. Firstly, we're talking about a group of individuals who self-isolate, seldom socialise and generally prefer the company of cats or dogs to other humans. So there's that.

The second challenge to creating a truly uplifting group of the six-sensed is to weed out the victimhood. I'll touch on this very gently now, for those ready to hear it.

There are two interpretations of 'Victimhood': The first is a statement of fact describing a moment in time where an incident included a persecutor, a victim. Possibly a fellow victim, and possibly a rescuer. These are labels to a moment in time to describe an event or series of events that took place.

The second interpretation of victimhood is when an individual, who possibly has been a real life victim of a particular incident wherein they WERE a victim, begins to identify themselves with Victimhood as a state of being. I call this the 'Pyramid of Pain' and its a horribly difficult mindset to break out of.

Within the Pyramid of Pain, the individual will label everyone they meet as either persecutor, fellow victim or potential rescuer. So pervasive is this ideology that the individual concerned wont even care about any additional details. So they are not really bothered with who other people are, what they believe or what makes them tick.

All they are interested in is what side of the triangle you fit on. Are you their Persecutor, Potential Rescuer or Fellow victim? They will even get mad if you don't co-operate with their labelling and behave in an inconsistent way. So if they have labelled you as a Rescuer, and you don't for some reason rescue them, then you will be automatically reassigned to Persecutor and become subject to all their defences and possibly their wrath. The Pyramid of Pain is immersed in blame – everything in the world from it being too hot, too cold or the state of the world is someone's fault. Sometimes it is. But the Pyramid of Pain victim is consistently surrendering their power to anyone and everyone else and therefore they are wholly disempowered to change their life or perspectives.

With traumatic childhoods and usually carrying a burden of unhealed pain, a lot of the six-sensed have identified with victimhood and spend a lot of time whining about their 'cursed extra senses'.

So open gatherings of the six-sensed that attract enough of these victimhood-identified individuals wont create a wholesome and nurturing environment for everyone. Give those individuals some time and space to break out of their victimhood (which just takes one clear choice that they take 100% responsibility for) – and a little further down their healing journey they will be wonderful to include in any gathering, but initially you need to be aware of this dynamic to assemble a group of six-sensed individuals who can truly support and uplift one another.

And no, you cannot extract anyone from the Pyramid of Pain. Its something that can ONLY be done by the individual themselves. (Even the rescuers need to extract themselves and cant be rescued from this trap. Rescuer is a point of identification in this pyramid remember, so people that are constantly 'rescuing' others can also be living this unhealthy ideology, even if they think they are the 'good guys' within it.)

The path to creating a small collective of like-minded others is simply to SEE it. Harness the power of attraction and visualise the kind of circle you would like to attract. Imagine being at one of your get-togethers, the deep and meaningful conversations you will have: What will that feel like? What would it feel like to be with a group of individuals who have the potential to truly see one another? Understand one another? Be there for each other on a path to exploring their senses and understanding what it is to be a new level of human?

If you wish to gather a group of six-sensers to be a support for one another, this is the method I would use – and then wait to encounter those individuals with a sign hanging over their head showing you 'include me!'.

It might take some trial and error, but this will get you most directly to the outcome you desire.

As an additional support for this process, I have installed the Indigo Rose groups, linked through my social media, where individuals that resonate with at least part of this information can find each other. There will be an entry process and whining will not be encouraged, but perhaps from there you can start to find your tribe.

Guidance for daily living

Where to from here?

The starting point has to be within our own selves. Take a moment to chew on this new perspective on the world. See how many people you can remember encountering who thought they had one or other 'illness' or imbalance but were possibly just six-sensed and didn't know it.

To the five sensed we ARE aberrant. We are a phenomenon to be tempered, reduced, brought back to 'normal' and so their efforts to do so will continue. However we can know that there is nothing in us to 'fix', but any indigo-born will have a road of healing ahead.

First we have to forgive them ALL. Society, our carers, siblings, friends and parents for not seeing us, and not understanding what we were dealing with. As five-sensed people, they could not know.

Then we need to become our own parent, friend and carer and begin to take really good care of ourselves. Accept that there is a way forward, not only to a tolerable life but to one full of joy, and that you CAN get there. You are supported by the love of thousands in the next world, and even if you NEVER have direct and meaningful contact with them, you can accept their help and support as you help and support them on their journey by living your best life.

If you can understand that

a – you are a six-sensed being in a five-sensed society and

b – all life is energy MANIFESTING into the world of being, with spirit giving life to it all,

then you will never truly feel alone again. You WILL know how very much you are loved and how you have all the guidance and support you will ever need right with you, at all times.

Your sixth sense will guide you gently and surely to a life that is comfortable, safe and peaceful and will help you to heal along the way.

There is another element to healing ourselves that directly serves the world, without any effort on our part.

There is a saying that family lines accumulate a lot of damage along the way, being passed down through cell memory or written into our energetic experiences of our families, and that at some point, an individual manifests into their human experience on that line to heal it. I've seen a lot of that over my lifetime. The worst and most broken family lineages often yield powerful six-sensed individuals who feel called to the field of healing.

If those individuals, take a course or two and become practitioners of a healing form, then that does not accomplish the work that Eudaemonic Resonance is intending (the natural flow of life to make whole, better and happy). If however that individual HEALS – goes on a healing journey, finds the broken parts of them that echo through the family lineage, THEN their mere presence in the family will bring healing to that line.

Remember, its all energy, everything has a frequency. And just as an illness had a frequency, so too does the healing of that illness or dis-ease have a frequency. One who internalises that healing for themselves, can then become a source of healing for all, simply through their presence.

In no way am I saying that the six-sensed should NOT follow a healing path in their work in the world, it's an admirable profession and much needed today. But there is a vacuous trend for people to go into healing or wellness of one kind or another, and practice the physical works and follow the guidebook on others, but skip over themselves – as if by healing enough others, healing will rub off on them.

In the traditional practice of Reiki (not the fast-food kind that takes a day to obtain a certificate as a Master), you cannot NOT apply the healing to yourself. Daily self-treatment is a part of the path to wholeness, for yourself, and by the time you achieve practitioner level, if you have an honourable Sensei, you will already be far along your own healing journey.

As a six-sensed individual, practising any kind of healing work is intense. All who come to you will echo something in yourself that is healed (and therefore being reinforced and shared), or unhealed and in need of attention. As a healing practitioner your own healing journey grows exponentially with each client – but to fully appreciate and get the most out of that practice for you and your clients, you must be starting at a balanced and level place in yourself – therefore again – "Healer, heal thyself" (first).

But being six-sensed doesn't automatically mean you'll be called to a healing path, so then you need to look about for healing practices that you can use as tools for your own wholeness and well-being.

My personal experience of living as a six-sensed being has ebbed and flowed throughout my life. I know that my system of belief kept me sane through much turbulence and constant questioning of everything was a great asset. I never stopped asking questions – both outwardly and inwardly, feeling my way to truth even if my mind couldn't see the path yet.

My early initiation into the healing art of Traditional Usui Shiki Rhoyo Reiki was key to healing early childhood damage and setting me on the path to rebalancing in life.

I had beautiful guides, both physical and 'non', who have helped me along the way to the point where I can now stand in my six-sensed clarified KNOWING of this aspect of the human experience.

Where you go from here is entirely up to you, but I would like to suggest you sit with this information and these perspectives a while, and see how it changes the world around you and your memories of the life you've lived so far. From this vantage-point, you may be able to see the damage you've incurred from a new perspective.

Misunderstanding of or resistance to the sixth sense might be at the core of a lot of your pain, but if you know that you chose to manifest into the world today – on the leading edge of human evolution – as a six-sensed human being – you can come to accept that damage as battle-scars of a war that must be waged in order for mankind to heal – and that you CHOSE to come here now to be a part of this next leap in humanity.

Knowing this truth, and how long it took your spiritual journey to arrive at this point of human manifestation, might be all the shift you need to get out there and start eeking the JOY from life that you came here for.

For some the two giant hurdles of DESERVING and RECEIVING will still to be vanquished before they allow joy back into the room, but they are merely shadow-monsters that can be dispelled with a little light.

Deserving:

Indigo Children seldom got the care they needed. This is obvious as the five-sensed carers would never have understood what was needed. This results in a belief that we don't deserve. It can even be written in our subconscious as an element of our Personal Law – the first five things we believed about ourselves as children.

There are a lot of deep and meaningful processes you can employ to unlock your deserving. Really its just a line of junk code inserted to protect your relationship with your carers and as an adult self, you can sit with your child self and, in the role of a parent to your own self, explain it to them gently.

Often simple imagery can dispel errant personal law and for deserving, breath is a powerful one.

Here you are and one of the most important actions that sustains your human existence is breath. Your breath sustains you, it keeps you alive. And it has done from the moment of your birth and your very first breath.

If life was determined in any way by deserving, then you would have needed to earn that first breath and you did not. You arrived and breath was freely available to you. What if all life is like that?

Make room for that possibility.

Receiving:

Once we open up to the possibility of deserving all that we need – or that deserving it is not in any way linked to receiving it, the next hurdle is usually receiving.

This is a vastly underrated and misunderstood state of being that can be the key to stepping into the life we have always wanted.

Everything worth having, is actively received at some level of our being.

Oxygen is required for life, but we need to breathe it in, absorb it, receive it. Life is like that too.

Do you see the problem?

The Indigo Adult has spent a lifetime damming up their receptors of everything. Information incoming on the sixth sense, scrutiny of others when they are trying hard to hide their true nature, other peoples feelings, the wrongness of so much 'out there' – running about in themselves slamming windows doors and portals SHUT is more the trend than the openness it would require to actively RECEIVE.

And yet love, even freely given, must be actively RECEIVED to be experienced. Trust, truth, guidance – all these things require an active receptor to 'hit home' and so closed portals, high walls and a moat full of crocs are going to be obstacles to welcoming anything.

There is a process I use with clients that helps enormously with opening, safely and gently, the right receptors, and again its about breath.

There is a mantra I use:

"As I breathe I receive"

and using this will get you started. If you understand that as you breathe in, you are receiving the very essence of life, freely and safely, and you wrap that action in consciousness – that can gently begin to open you up to receiving other good things.

You were always receiving is the point, your consciousness can sift and sort the good stuff from the rest and so you can trust yourself to receive all that is to your benefit.

There is a very rudimentary visualisation that I used to use when I started out. That of creating a bubble around me when I went anywhere. I had heard that pink was a healing colour and so I imagined the bubble to be a clear pink one, that would allow in only what was nurturing and healing. If you repeated that visualisation everyday for 60 days, it would become habit and you will carry it with you from then on.

This bubble lets in light, good information, uplifting thoughts, all things yay and yummy, but it keeps out unwanted energies, frequencies and information.

When you use this visualisation, you are really just cementing the intention to tune to all that supports your process and your well-bring, and tune out all that does not, and by harnessing this visualisation everyday for a period of time, you will make this state your default.

Six-sensed children are fantastic at working with this kind of process and you can use this type of visualisation to create a place of safety and openness to work with six-sensed children that will serve them meaningfully their whole lives. Initially you would invite them into your bubble, and then teach them to create bubbles of their own. This then can be their first step to tuning their receptors to receive good, positive and nurturing information – rather than all the noise that is coming at them.

Wrap yourself in a comfortable bubble of love, protection and safety and then allow yourself to receive within that filtered space.

The practical doings:

Language and understanding

Think for a moment of the sixth sense as any other sense. Sight for example. You are born and you SEE. That sight develops clarity as you live into a world that agrees: that set of frequencies is called purple and that set, red. This is LIGHT and that is DARK.

For the five senses there are existing grids. We receive visual information and there's already a name in place for it! Yay! And so we can label that and communicate about it simply and easily with anyone who speaks our language.

No such grid exists for the sixth sense. We continue to hijack five-sensed terminology to try to stretch that out as far as possible to cover what we are experiencing.

For a sense that even Western medicine accepts that 25% of people have, that's a little odd, but nevertheless we have to make it up as we go.

What I've learnt to do, so as not to get caught up on terminology, is to feel for what another person is trying to express, and then name it together. Our language will evolve to allow us accurate expression but for now its important to understand that the void in language of words to express the sixth sense aspects is vast, and many people have filled it in with terminology that may differ from person to person.

Know that you experience life differently to most other humans, you 'feel' more, you 'see' more and you experience life at a whole new level of being.

The first step for a self-aware six-senser, as is the process in the development of a toddler, is to figure out where you end and the rest of the world begins.

This sounds elemental but its at the core of what makes most six-sensed feel 'fragile' or off-balance.

Redefining YOU

A few years ago there was a global event and before many six-sensed became aware of the details of the event, the message boards and chat rooms were flooded with reports of people feeling and overwhelming sense of dread. Even when they personally were unafraid, still they experienced the dread that swept across the world, as if it were their own.

In my household, it is not uncommon for one of us to walk into a room and ask – "Who is craving lemon merengue pie?" (or any specific food). In my home, we are all aware of the shared band of energy and how information moves about within it. I don't like lemon merengue pie, so when I become aware of a craving for it, I know for sure that's coming from one of the other residents of my home.

Many years ago, I lived in a quaint area that was full of students and young people, just starting out, and a smattering of elderly folk. I lived in a flat and worked long hours managing a restaurant so was seldom home.

I liked the apartment, it was enough for my needs and the area had all I wanted. It served me very well for a time. One day when I was at work, new neighbours moved in to the apartment next door. I didn't meet them – my hours were odd and I didn't arrive or leave at normal times but I was aware that there were new people about.

On the odd occasion that I would spend more than a few hours at home, I started to become weepy and sad – without really having any reason behind it. There were no thoughts I could associate with the sadness, but once I began to feel that way, every experience I had ever had that was sad like that seemed to come up for me. It was a dreadfully depressing time.

My work suffered, although again, I could find absolutely no cause for the feelings except memories of sadness that were far distant. And then one weekend. The couple in the flat next door – the new neighbours, had a blow out raging fight and I could hear the beatings through the wall. The man stormed off but the woman was left alone, weeping.

I finally understood that all these weeks, it was not me that was sad, it was the woman in the flat next door and she was being beaten regularly.

It was such a marked incident that it clarified for me something I'd suspected all my life – that some or most of the things I would feel, if they didn't relate to a direct happening in MY life, were not actually my feelings at all, but I was picking up on the emotions of the woman who lived behind three inches of wall.

How many of the six-sensed go about their days on a roller-coaster of emotion? Picking this up here, that up there – the man besides them at the grocery store beaming lust, the woman in the car beside us, weeping, and then just as quickly, the child that beams up at us can fill us with glee. Its a mess. And until we learn to define what is OF us and what is OUT THERE, we're just quite literally a hot mess.

You have to start there. Even to know if thoughts feel good or not means clearing out what everyone else is feeling and honing in on YOUR own feelings.

The easiest thing is to move out to the countryside – put space between you and everyone else and that helps to turn down the 'noise' of other people. I've found that homes made of as much natural material as possible are best, so stone and thatch would be ideal, wood is good too - these elements dampen the noise. I will never again live in an apartment where there are people living behind a wall besides me, but if that isn't possible then there are natural elements that can help. Wool or silk hangings, stone tiles - natural materials that help to dampen the feelings from 'out there'.

And then you need to really know yourself. If a feeling of dread creeps in, you need to know if there was a thought you were thinking or something you saw just a moment ago that would have brought up dread for you, and if not, look around for someone else who could be feeling that way.

You and them. Learn what is yours and what you are simply picking up through your sixth sense. Awareness of this aspect of living as a six-sensed human is half the battle of mastery over yourself and will clean up a lot of the chaos of your emotional life.

(There is a process workbook available simply titled Me. My little black book of self-actualisation, that can support this process too so keep an eye open for that if you need added support in this area).

Have a daily practice:

As a Gen X'er I don't do well with 'must' or 'have to's but this one I've come to understand as vital. Let there be a time of the day where you go and sit somewhere and meditate for at least five minutes. If it can be the same environment even better.

Meditation too was a challenge for me. I have a busy mind and meditation seemed elusive. I found through Reiki, a form that is effortless for me, I slip right into Theta and meditate for as long as is needed that day.

There are many forms of meditation that work for many different people. Alpha meditation can be anything from running to gardening or knitting. The key is to have a quiet time with you when you can check-in with yourself and notice any shifts or changes. You might like to add a God or Source-element into this time like prayer or reading from Holy Writings, something to get your consciousness pointed in a specific direction, but this time, with you, is key to maintaining balance.

In this time, it is as if you are sitting, naked and alone with the rest of the universe and feeling for your place within it. During meditation you can receive beautiful insights, 'knowings' and downloads from Divine Intelligence that can help guide your next steps.

Equally as important, you will have a moment to feel if you are off-balance somehow and realign with what you want from your day rather than hopping onto the frequency of anything that is going wrong.

I urge clients to write down nine things each day that they love. Call those things to mind with detail. Try for nine new things everyday and just sit in the savouring of the memories of the experience of them. Meditation done in the state of love and appreciation can be delightful and uplifting.

I also encourage clients to write down three things each day that they want – and only in the positive. So if they want a comfortable and peaceful home, to focus on that, rather than focusing on not wanting the home they are in.

You can use one notebook to write these things in – front and back – and after 20 days, you will have a resource to turn to anytime you need it. If for example you're feeling 'down' or annoyed, you can turn to the pages of the things you love and recall all those yummy things, and this will help you shift your frequency from something that doesn't feel good, to something that feels much better.

After 20 days you also have a pure and shining foundation for understanding who you really are. You are not a human doing, you are spirit, having a human experience and in this experience, the clearest definition of who we really are is to be found in all the things we love. It is in calling to mind the things we love that most quickly and easily can shift us into higher and higher states of being where we can see and feel direct results of tuning into who we really are.

Your daily practice could be a walk you take in nature everyday, or a long soak in the tub where you catch up with you with no distractions. Whatever form calls to you, this practice will give you a moment to check in, feel for what is different today, identify if anything you're feeling is really coming FROM you, and soothe yourself by remembering that you are the result of the love of thousands and you are here on purpose, with a purpose, that will unfold before you gently, when you are ready.

Get off the cross, someone needs the wood

Too harsh? Well come now, its been long enough. The whining and complaining you hear from 'empaths' and other-labeled six-sensers is deafening if you dip your toe into any chat group or social media page or in person, to groups where many of our kind gravitate into.

"Why cant I just be normal?"

Well why cant you? You chose to be here, now, in this time and place as a six-sensed individual. Sure, there are challenges but cutting off your sixth sense now would be like someone removing your sight or your hearing.

You chose this moment, this time and place because you are a courageous spirit – reaching for the BEST, the MOST, the EVERYTHING of life. YOU did not want to settle for 'meh' because you KNEW you could rock this leading edge version of human experience. Trust that you knew that, trust that your Higher Self still KNOWS that and is excited about what you can still do with this one precious life. You can achieve more than you ever dreamed possible, starting now! Just not from a cross with nails in your appendages. Get those precious feet under you and TRUST yourself. You've got this!

Alone in a sea of normal

"What is it like to be you?" - is a question we don't hear enough. But the truth is no-one can really step into your experience. But if you are Indigo-born, then whether you know it or not, your sixth sense is as much a part of how you navigate life as any of your other five senses.

I was a teenager and developed a bleeding ulcer. It was a particularly challenging time for me and the medical folk decided I was 'sensitive', and should be taking little white pills to dull my sensitivity. I took the pill and got on the bus to school.

Within 10 minutes of that bus ride the world went silent. The bus was full of chattering people, that just a moment ago I had been able to FEEL, I had been able to sense their intentions, their dominant thoughts, what they were feeling now and what they felt about the world generally, and suddenly my view of the present was reduced to five-sensed input.
I knew right away that this was the effect of that little white pill. So I took them out of my bag and threw them out the window. It took a full eight hours for my senses to return, but I remember thinking clearly then, that I would need to find a way to be healthy without becoming someone else.

A life without your sixth sense might seem attractive if you're having a moment of feeling particularly sorry for yourself, but trust me, the hours I spent without it showed me that it can also be a living hell – like having your sense of touch removed. We would need to relearn to navigate the world, and we would have LESS information, not more.

I'm not unsympathetic, I know personally how tough it can be, but there are enough tools and guides and support structures out there now for it not to be the lonely road it once was.

Alyce Dylan

Start here:

I am a six-sensed human living in a five-sensed world, and its going to be alright.
I've made it to here and I am going to figure this out.
Its getting easier everyday.
I understand more about the world now and how it works and I'm getting this.
There is not now nor has there ever been anything wrong with me.

Tuning IN

You are really like a radio, that can receive on six wavelengths at the same time. What so many humans forget is that they are in control of the tuner!

So they walk unconsciously through the world with the preset of 'random', picking up everything that shows up before them and their lives are spent ping-ponging around frequencies which are for the most part determined by the world around them.

There is an older gentleman to whom we gave refuge a few years ago when he lost his life-partner and subsequently his home too, during the global shut-downs. He's a Boomer and his life is like this: Besides a few choices he actively makes, like where to play bowls on the weekend and what work he does (he grooms animals), the rest of life seemingly happens TO him.

I often take him with me on errands if he needs to get somewhere and it's on the way. Sitting in the car he will read out random words he sees – from the makes of vehicles we pass to the names of shops or the bill-boards we drive past.

He will also jump on and complain loudly about bad drivers, careless pedestrians or taxi drivers. It has never occurred to him that the content of his life is largely determined by what he CHOOSES to pay attention to.

I've tried gently to suggest he spend just one week looking for all the good things in the world, but the momentum he has running in his life is all about what's wrong with everything – and of course therefore for him, things go wrong a lot.

It's unlikely he will change at this stage, but he's a genuinely nice human being with a good heart and a series of things going right for him, may help him to shift perspective to tune into a more positive picture.

Turn the dial.

If heavy mental is not what you want to be listening to today, tune to the classical channel.

The HOW is easy. Find a memory, or visualise a scene, in which you are peaceful, flowing, blissful. Life felt GOOD. People were nice. Or a memory of a successful time when you achieved a great victory in life. Immerse yourself in the feeling, scents, sounds and energy of that moment.

Ahhhh. Feels good right?

If you struggle initially with this, you can go to your I LOVE list and just skim through all the things you love – that will also tune you to a nice, high frequency.

And then notice how much lines up with just that frequency through your day.

At first you might need to do this a few times a day, stop, retune and continue, but the outcomes will soon convince you that YOU have the power to tune into higher frequencies and then your attention will flow towards events and vistas that align with that frequency.

Add broadcasting that frequency to this practice and you'll have a meaningful effect on everyone you encounter while broadcasting your chosen frequency of love, contentment, peace or prosperity and success.

Remember the radio and know that if what you are seeing or noticing through your day is a series of things which DON'T line up with how you'd LIKE to be feeling, then that's an early warning to switch frequencies. Purposefully LOOK for beauty, peace and ease. See the delighted child skipping down the road, notice the flowers in bloom, fulfilling their life purpose, and with some small adjustments, you can shift the momentum of the moment enough that what shows up for you next will be events and situations that ARE pleasing and uplifting.

The 'HOW TO GET AHEAD IN LIFE' practices, have to be really simple. It would not seem just to me that a spirit manifesting into the human experience in the stone age should be greatly disadvantaged by time as someone born today.

The 'how-to's' of this time and space reality surely have to be equitable to those of by-gone eras and so they have to be really really simple. Any all-knowing creator HAS to know how easy it was going to be to get lost in this human experience and so the guidebook is hardwired into our very Being.

If it feels stretchy, struggly and hard, then at the very least we need to stop and reassess, if not change direction entirely. What is right for us FEELS right, it FEELS good, it is effortless and comfortable – even if what Is right for us in that moment is to walk through a lesson that we really need to get to the other end of for our lives to improve.

This is true for all human experience, not just the six-sensed. For us its just amplified and ON in every moment. The only detraction can be the noise 'out there' before we learn how to define and bubble ourselves securely.

What could be easier than actively LOOKING for things to appreciate, to marvel out, to admire about this world? A cave-man could do that. And if he did, more things just like that would turn up in his experience because he's tuned to THAT frequency.

You are actively in control of this bit. YOU get to tune to the frequencies and energies that are pleasing to you and once you are practised in tuning in, you can also beam that energy outward.

Your life will get easier quickly and showing up each day will become an adventure.

Nature Rocks!

There's no space healthier for the six-sensed than out in nature. Preferably barefoot. (Look up Grounding, its a practice that makes so much sense for electrical beings as we all are.

Five minutes everyday with your bare feet on the earth should do it – you will feel the difference right away.)

Natural vistas can calm our spirits, reconnect us with beauty, nature and animals have a clearer and calming energy about them. They have a purpose, an intent, they are getting on with the business of being a tree or a dog or even an insect and most are doing a great job.

Sitting in nature reminds us of all the natural laws at work. Water flows, air circulates, trees reach upward. There are very few life principles not reflected somewhere in the natural order of the world and when we sit in a natural environment, surrounded by natural law, we are reassured that there is something greater than all of us at work here.

There are laws that guide the unfolding of life, clearly and beautifully. Everything has a function and a place and everything works together to create harmony.

It is only in the human world where the fake is embraced and the world is forced to someone's will, that feels wrong and chaotic to us. This wears on our being like sandpaper until we return to somewhere in nature and just reconnect with the world we manifested into as human beings.

The 6-sensed are greatly refreshed and invigorated by spending time in natural environments, often and on purpose. When we hug trees, we benefit enormously! Try it!

Understanding frequency

So, Quantum Physics tells us that all 'stuff' is really energy and that's a significant understanding that mankind has arrived at. So we broke things down and broke things down to their smallest possible parts (that we could perceive) and we find – energy. Not matter at all.

The role of the observer has also been quantified. In experiments where particle accelerators have been used to observe these minute particles of energy, we have seen that some of these particles only appear when observed – by the human eye or by human attention.

So things are not things at all but energy, and some of the things ONLY pop into existence under the condition of human observation – which confirms that there is something about our observation of life, our attention TO this or that, that influences matter.

When these experiments were conducted therefore, when a human being was present and observing, some elements would appear and when the experiments were conducted unobserved – but still recorded, those same elements would not appear.

The power of our observation or attention is more profound than we have ever understood and so too is the power of withdrawing our attention from something.

I think at some level we all get that our attention is powerful, but we misunderstand how that truly works. You see most of humanity running about paying loads of attention to everything that is going wrong – and yes, there is some crossing of wires there through the impulse to bring issues into the light so that those issues might be cleansed by illumination. But more often than not, our attention to all that is wrong simply enhances the wrongness and gives it momentum.

Objective, unfettered investigation of truth is key, but in order to fix anything, more attention needs to be added to the solution of the issue than to the problem.

Apply this understanding then to your now-present human reality. You've lived a bit of life, you've accumulated lessons and information about the world. Some of it good, a lot of it not so pleasing – and now the impulse in the generality of mankind is to root about in everything that is wrong with your wiring so far, and pick apart all the happenings that resulted in the faulty wiring in order to fix that.

Well that's like needing to interview the original installer (s) of an electrical system in a house that's been badly wired to correct faults showing up today. It's also tied into this assumption of backwards reality – where it is assumed that all emotional or spiritual growth will emerge out OF physical reality and so if there's a problem – the solution sits in the physical. And that is just not the case.

You are a spiritual being having a human experience within a physically manifested 'stage' of being – all perfectly laid out for your ideal learning, growing and playfully expansive experience – but the stuff is not who you are and you did not come from stuff. Yes, as far as it goes all matter comes from 'dust' and will return to 'dust', but YOU are the manifestor of all that dust into a human vehicle for this human experience.

A portal opened at the moment of conception and you jumped in, and it was YOUR presence that gave life to the manifesting form. The form obeys YOU. It responds to YOUR thoughts and feelings. As much as there are alchemical processes born of the DNA you harness, you are still steering the ship.

If you live in fear or uncertainty, your body WILL pad itself against the potential danger. When you feel safe, secure and aligned, the need for the padding will dissipate. This vehicle is magnificent as it responds to each and every shift and adjustment in your perspective and your understanding of the world and it is always responding to YOU.

As long as you continue to believe that this body is some accident of nature upon which you are hitching a ride but it is ultimately affected by and conditioned by outside conditions, you will be allowing the influence of outside forces. But when you understand that YOU are the driver, that the object under your fingertips is the steering wheel, then you reclaim your true power. But that can feel like too heavy a responsibility for most people and they prefer to give their power away to physicians or food or the government.

We don't have to consciously, intellectually KNOW everything about these bodies as a six-sensed beings because we have access to the guidance of al those who have gone before us, to the frequency of truth and the energies of health and wholeness. There are also laws and principles that we can feel the flow of, but that's a more complex subject.

So we don't have to know exactly what actions will result in health and wholeness, merely tune into the energies of that BE-ingness and the right actions for US, will show up – either in our environment or through our own being.

A student of mine kept craving Kimchee: a Korean fermented food that he had eaten a lot of in New Zealand and he missed and craved more of it. It isn't a food that is available where he now lives, in fact its quite hard to find. The only versions you are likely to find are full of chillies, which he doesn't like and so his partner got a little ruffled over his consistent call for a food she could not find and was unlikely to come across.

His muscles started spasming and no physician could find a cause for that and eventually he went into heart failure – which fortunately was caught and since he lives a life of faith and alignment, he came through the experience and is still on his journey to wholeness.

Looking back however, what we now know is that Kimchee contains large amounts of vitamin K2 that is vital for heart and muscle health and so his persistent and even annoying craving for a food that was not available – if it had been answered, could possibly have prevented his heart failure.

When we understand everything as energy operating at different frequencies, with those frequencies being interpreted through our limited grids – if we are paying exquisite attention – we can catch impulses at an early stage and really hear them.

I'm going to push the analogy of the vehicle here to a new level of understanding for those who have kept up so far. So we pop through this portal of existence into a magical moment of conception where DNA meets other DNA in an ideal environment and we give life to that manifestation which then kicks off a series of happenings that results in development, expansion and growth of a human BE-ing.

From the moment we start having thoughts and responses to our environment, that vehicle which IS us, but not ONLY us and not ALL of us, responds and adjusts to the new impulses, intentions and frequencies.

So as much as we are not ONLY the vehicle – our true being is spirit – but that spirit is focused ON and is giving life to this vehicle – but is also separate from it as an artist is separate from their art. The artist pours themselves INTO their art, to mix with the materials of the paint, the canvass, the clay or the wood – and so their art IS their creation, but it is not THEM.

Just as when our physical selves sleep, our spirit-selves are free to travel, in space and time – and have experiences – that are sometimes brought back to our human experience as certain types of dreams, and so our true spiritual selves are not dependent on this physical form, but are rather living INTO this human experience through these physical manifestations.

So too, our vehicle for living this human experience is not US, but it is OF us, and it is our expression into the world of creation. But who is driving?

Well for the first few years, our parents are really. Our human self is responding to their likes and dislikes or rules and so they are really determining our path at first until our human self – a composite of our intellectual, emotional and spiritual impulses – matures and takes the wheel.

For the five-sensed, all the developmental truisms about teenage and young adulthood now apply. We identify ourselves as separate and adopt a series of ethics and principles and if we now live in accordance with those ethics and principles, happiness is possible.

The six-sensed individual has a further choice at this point – if they have by now established enough trust in and alignment with their spirit-selves, their intuitive or extra-sensory connection, they can hand the wheel of the 'vehicle' back to their Higher Selves and instead ride 'shot-gun' or upfront passenger in the human experience, allowing their Higher or Spirit Selves that has access to the intuitive knowing and wisdom of all who went before to truly be driving, but from their vantage-point upfront they can navigate, express preferences and have more attention for observing.

When this happens, even when they say – turn right here – if the higher self knows there's a dead end or a great big pot-hole on the right-turn path, life will proceed forward, but short of any danger the Higher Self is aware of, the human self is in charge of this experience.

However because of the difficulties – in this age – inherent in the development path of the Indigo Child, its more likely – for now – that the Human Self (ego) of the developing six-sensed human – will take the wheel. Without listening to the guidance of their Higher self, they will need to take a lot of detours, a lot of wrong turns and circles around until they finally get to the place of asking how to put their Higher Self INTO the drivers seat, so they can move over and have more fun, observe more and focus more on where they WANT to be going.

But just as it isn't necessary at this point to somehow go back in time and install their Higher Selves into the driver seat at the coming of age – just like it isn't necessary from here to go digging around in history for all that went wrong and try to fix it on a place in the time-line to which this physical reality is fixed, all rectification is possible, right from here, if we align with the true source of everything – the energy of it.

TO stretch this analogy even further then, if you find yourself driving around Paris when you really wanted by now to be in Kinshasa but took so many detours from your human ego decision-making processes – all you would need to do now is visualise the successful completion of the journey to Kinshasa, your glee at arriving there safely, and your Higher Self would get you there. Yes there would be a journey ahead, you may need to watch for road signs and respond to impulses as they turned up, but with your true eternal spiritual self at the wheel, your arrival where you really want to be is assured.

For the six-sensed human, that aligns with their true eternal spiritual self, is receiving guidance constantly from their Higher Self and is getting their ego out of the way of interpretation of that information and following that guidance as they themselves learn and upload that learning to their also-expanding spiritual self, life can be an effortless experience of joy and glee – punctuated only by opportunities to learn about something new or broaden their experience. Life is rich, intense and ecstatic and the WHOLE of you, your physical human vehicle self, your intellectual-emotional ego self and your Higher or spiritual self are all together enriched and heightened by all of it.

Comparatively, the five-sensed human experience would stop at the emergence of the ego-self and be able to reach into alignment with their true, spiritual self only through activities like prayer or meditation – which hopefully in time would awaken the sixth sense and that channel would stabilise and they too would be able to give the wheel over to their Higher Selves. But as five-sensed humans, they are in constant need of INTERVENTION – so calling on Source, through Its operation through high vibrational Beings, to intervene in their path to guide or direct their next steps.

As six-sensed humans, that guidance is always available to us and prayer and meditation will merely enhance and amplify it – as well as keeping it directed at the highest possible Source of guidance and Good.

Wave-forms

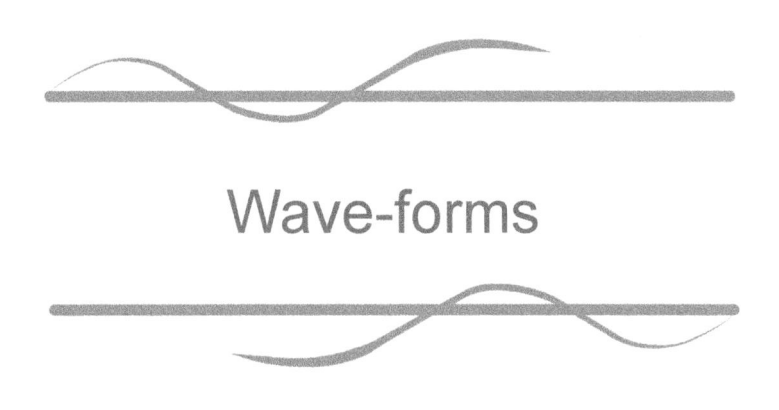

Understanding frequency then is simplest through those experiments you may have done at school when you drop objects in pools of water – which creates waves. So the action of the object impacting the water creates a wave that ripples outwards.

Energy vibrates at various frequencies and we can see the effect of those frequencies in the same way we see waves, when a frequency intersects with another.

The information we are receiving all the time through our sixth sense is also energetic, at various frequencies and we then become the interpreters of that energy into information, knowing or thought.

We've all had the experience of receiving information that is so clear and true, that we feel physically impacted by it. It causes a ripple. It can take us time to fully digest new information received, sometimes requiring a reshuffling of other held beliefs or thoughts which no longer align with the reality we now know to be true.

This is the reason why many individuals experience impact or life-shuffle as a result of taking up meditation or stepping into a new spiritual path – as they quiet their ego self and allow space for their true eternal spiritual self to connect with their created reality, the frequencies that download to their human awareness can impact that state of Being, causing ripples. Spiritual paths, harnessing a direct connection with Source can have a staggering effect as we open up the channels to higher and higher frequencies, the effect of those frequencies in our lives can seem devastating, but are always only a clearing away of what is no longer in alignment with new now-reality.

It follows then that as we open ourselves to higher and higher frequencies, our own state of being elevates too – as frequencies that meet each other will equalise, with the lower always being elevated.

A dear friend has a grandfather who was in human life and still is in spirit, a spiritual dynamo. In life he was an exemplar of a meaningful Spiritually guided life, and after leaving his human form behind he was already at a very high frequency and has no doubt elevated since then.

This friend is six-sensed and receives clear dreams amongst other forms of communication and in one dream, his Grandfather came to him to set him straight on some subjects. In the dream he explained how he didn't have much time because it was not a simple thing for him to lower his own vibration enough to be able to communicate at a level that our friend could receive.

SO as we grow and learn, as we progress as spirit, our frequencies raises and our lives sometimes – as an emanation of the frequency of our current reality – need to adjust to any adjustment in our frequency.

In my young-adulthood I spent some time with a group of people who would 'sit circle' weekly and connect with souls in the next world. It was an interesting experience for me because I had never had the opportunity to explore my sixth sense with any group of people before. As time went on, I came to understand that the souls that turned up at these circles really didn't have that much to offer any of us. Sure, they had some expanded perspectives they shared, but in deep questions of life and death, they would seldom give us anything of significant value. SO in the next plane too, there are stages or levels of growth. I came to unpick the understanding I'd picked up from society at large that when we cross over to the next plane, we suddenly have access to all knowledge and wisdom. We don't. Some souls in the next world can know less than we do on certain subjects, although certainly they are seeing life from an elevated perspective – but they are still on their own journey towards Source too.

Souls who have recently passed over, or ones on the other side that did little in terms of spiritual growth on this plane, are closer in frequency to us and therefore are often on our 'bandwidth'. They can assist our lives by holding their attention on our highest good or focusing on the healing of an aspect of the family line. We serve them simply by living our best lives, and in accompanying us along our path they continue to learn and grow vicariously through us.

But those who elevate significantly and move further along the spiritual path elevate out of the frequency that is on our 'bandwidth', and need to 'level down' to a bandwidth closer to us in order to communicate with us. The higher the frequency of our thoughts and focus, the more elevated the souls that we have access to.

Said another way, just because they leave their human experience does not mean they now have all the answers to life, the universe and everything. For those, you'll need to reach far higher frequencies.

There are exceptions to this, souls who are at the highest frequency of being and are in service to Good. Some call these beings Angels – my spiritual path names them 'The Concourse'. These beings are those that answer our calls for assistance or who show up in response to passionate prayers for aid and they carry a whopper! I experience them as beings of pure light who emanate powerfully the energies of love, healing, justice or protection.

A neighbour of ours is a spiritual practitioner herself, in an entirely different tradition, that I have had many hours of delightful conversation and sharing with, finding the meeting-places in our understanding of how our sixth sense works and our role in all of it.

In our time of sharing her 'faeries' have given me great gifts that I am deeply appreciative of, and I have initiated her into Reiki which she now uses in her practice.

While we are – in our human experience – sharing and exchanging and forging new understandings across cultural and traditional lines, I am intensely aware that our ancestry are also exchanging information at their level, sharing memories, experiences and knowing.

At one point she became embroiled in a conflict with a practitioner that she had shared part of her journey with, as they went down a darker and lower vibrational path while she kept reaching upwards towards better and clearer and more whole. She was shocked by this fellow-travellers detour down a darker path and initially tried to resist it – almost on his behalf – as if her resistance would somehow deter him, which of course it would not. Her distress however was real and manifested in various ways – especially around her home, where she still had items he had given her.

I was happy to do what I could to help, although in my path there are no dark forces or possibilities to misuse the sixth sense, I reasoned that by filling her space with light, love and higher frequencies, we should be able to cleanse it of most of what was ailing her.

So we set about creating a Reiki circle with her and a few of my students and offered high-powered prayers into and through that circle for cleansing of the space and release from bondage of the participants.

To my complete shock – THREE members of The Concourse showed up and hovered about our circle. Amidst my focus on the process we were holding, I almost apologetically spoke with one of them asking why they were there? Yes, we were asking for assistance, sure, but what we were addressing hardly warranted such high-powered intervention – surely?

He explained to me that there was a very significnt issue at the heart of what we were addressing and that they had been waiting for someone to ask, for them to intervene.

We completed our asking and ceremony and went away feeling altered and impacted by the experience. My neighbour felt relieved that something had shifted. But in the following weeks she became aware of far-flung happenings – followers of this other practitioner awakening from comas, break-ups of small groups of what the west would call 'cults' and she knew these things were in response to the intervention we had all asked for on her behalf.

Our intention was simple, authentic and gentle, but our asking had an effect far beyond our small gathering.

These Concourse members then, in my experience, respond to requests, they don't seem to be able to act unless asked and they honour the Free Will of all those involved. But when anyone is being genuinely victimised, it is in their power to free souls from bondage.

God-focused prayer then points a channel directly at the Source of all light and love and what we send upwards might be piddling but what comes back at us through that channel is the very stuff of life.

Focus therefore on our Ancestry is good, it will open a channel to them at the vibration they are at and the result will be raising our own vibrational frequency, but opening a channel – even WITH them, to the Source of all light and love, raises the frequency of us all.

In a small gathering of people too, awareness of frequency can assist you to understand human dynamics. If one individual is operating at a very high frequency and is in joy, bliss or glee, but one other of the group is at a very low frequency, exuding hopelessness, resentment and anger, either all these will equal out and the group will end up somewhere in the middle – or those at the opposite ends of the frequency will conflict in some way, usually with the one at the lower frequency trying to drag the other down to their level.

If we learn to elevate our vibration and hold it steady in love, appreciation or peace, those at a different frequency will either be elevated by our presence or be held away from interacting with us – OR, if we are not steady, interacting with them will exhaust us as we try to maintain our high elevation.

There is a woman at a shop I visit who is just one of half a dozen servers there. Her being overflows with resentment, distaste and seeping rage. I've often allowed other people past me in the queue just to avoid interacting with her.

On other days, when I'm soaring in bliss, love and appreciation for life, I know I will not encounter her, and indeed I do not. Even if I am next and she is ready to help someone, something will happen to call her away and one of the others will serve me. But when I am anywhere near the vibration of her low state of being, I need to manipulate events to steer clear of interacting with her.

As an Intuitive Counsellor, I am deeply aware of the frequency of our beings and how, in counselling others, we need to at least offer solutions which align with the frequency or state of being they are on, in order to be of service to them.

If someone comes to see me and is deeply depressed and sad, surrounding them with joy and bliss will just annoy them. You cant get to joy from depression. So we start with acceptance, relief and hope and can slowly nudge them along the emotional scale to a better-feeling vibration.

The same is true for social interactions – understand that if you arrive to visit with a group of friends where one is sad and depressed, your appreciation and joy wont be welcome at that moment. But if you can offer THEM acceptance and relief, or some hope, then you will avoid needing to step completely off your high vibration as a natural response to interacting with them.

This can be why many six-sensed individuals end up in the healing profession. We feel the shifts in vibration, feel the frequencies meet, settle and shift and so if we bring some conscious awareness to these interactions, we can be of great service to those living unconscious lives as we guide them – either through conversation or some practice, to a higher vibrational state. Most have learned to do this organically and therefore the result is a skilled healer, following their inner guidance, being of service in the world.

As far as mediumship goes however, the most likely contact we will make when we work with an individual will be to their family, their ancestral line. These individuals may be 'living with' an individual, focusing on their highest good, offering guidance – even if it's not received – and can give us insight into an individuals' day-to-day challenges or obstacles.

But these 'faeries' are not the source of all wisdom – for that you will need to reach to far higher frequencies AND, you would need to be ready to receive the answers that come back, or you will not be able to interpret or translate them.

'Guides' are interesting. There are many souls about whose lines died at some disaster or catastrophic event, and so they gravitate to individuals living lives that contain elements they are interested in, or where their knowing can be of service. They can be from distant lands but the life of the individual they choose to 'walk besides' holds appeal for them both in what they can contribute and what they still need to learn.

Said another way, for your spiritual truths and soul-quests, you will still need a spiritual path. Your guides, ancestors and helpers can help your journey immensely, but they are all on their own journey too – just a little further along.

So let us imagine for a moment that there is a 'bandwidth' around the human experience. At the lowest end of the frequencies we have the human animal experience – governed by instinct, survival and reasoning – right through to light-beings of incredible power and insight, having shifted their focus back to spirit, endowed with a Soul and really rocking truth, grace, service and joy. Everywhere in between is where we play in our human experience – and even after the physical bit is over.

On the animal end, it can seem simple with clean lines, survive, thrive, get ahead. Or it can be chaotic and dramatic.

The Spiritual side of the curve connects into spiritual 'reality'. At first through intention, turning 'spirit-ward' and then through the activation of the sixth sense, we expand our faculty to perceive the realm of spirit – while still grounded in the physical. Here we can be of great benefit to our ancestry as we work with them to heal ancestral damage in our lineages, supporting their progress in the "next world" as they support ours.

I'll state again, for anyone a little nervous, that you never need to have an encounter with anyone you thought of as 'dead' – they know how you feel and will never impose themselves on you. You need simply ask if you wish to limit your experience of them. But that will not prevent you from receiving guidance through 'intuition' or 'knowing'.

Having a sixth sense might put us on the leading edge of human evolution – but someone raised five-sensed could awaken tomorrow and without resistance or historical damage to deal with, they can soar through the realms of spirit and become a spiritual power-house. There is no space for arrogance on our journey.

Like the plants, the animals and the bees, we can just reach for 'the light', seek healing, comfort, peace and happy, and Eudaemonic resonance will take us to our next steps and the perfect next steps from there. Everyone has their own pace and each their own path. I revel in the awe I feel witnessing the trajectories of my students, clients and friends as they launch themselves into this work and soar.

When I first meet many of them they are ill, broken, lost or unbalanced and through embracing the truth of their being, and then connecting to and then following their inner guidance they rocket ahead into vistas of joy and purpose that they never could have imagined before.

There are no limits to how GOOD life can get when you harness your sixth sense to work FOR you.

The Impact of technology

Besides the effects of EMF and radiation, that still is not fully understood in the world, you have to understand that if your sixth sense is energetic, it is not limited by space and time. So if you hop onto the internet and join in a conversation with 100 others, you are now in direct contact with those others through your sixth sense.

Whereas the five-sensed use technology as a convenience, as six-sensed we have to understand the additional impact of the sixth sense through technology.

If the six-sensed felt overwhelmed just with the 100 or so exposures everyday of people they passed on the way to work, people in their workplace and at the stores, that level of overwhelm has now quadrupled with the advent of the internet and chat rooms across all social media.

During those times when you need to comfort yourself, self-isolate and regroup, it is not enough to simply stay home, you would also need to stay offline too.

The impact (and I mean impact because the effect is visceral for the six-sensed) of participating in a chat room with 100 others can be just the same as going to a teeming restaurant. Those tendrils going out to everyone are still creating the link, you will still receive the information and because it seems one step away, its less obvious that really what you are feeling is coming from someone at the other end of your internet connection.

Take clear steps to manage that space as you would in your physical world. Just don't expose yourself to all the anger, hatred and ick! I have such clear social media 'rules' for myself. I use the space to broadcast OUT – kindness, truth and well-being and NEVER entertain anything that doesn't feel interesting at least, joyous at best.

It can be a space to connect with like-minded others, but you will either elevate those you encounter to your frequency or be brought down by those at a lower frequency – just like meeting in person. It's up to you to choose which you will allow.

Remember first that technology is a creation, and it needs to Serve us first and foremost. We are the co-creators, the intenders, the visionaries. Any technological advancement that seeks to free humanity, enrich lives and allow information to flow has a place in this world. Anything other than just that, does not.

The sixth sense and imagination

It's no coincidence that 'seeing' is experienced just like a day-dream, but one where you are not the author of the 'dream'. The parts of the brain that are of the highest frequency and therefore are the receptors of our extra-sensory perception, are also the parts of the brain that activate when we visualise, day-dream or imagine.

What mankind has so far failed to grasp is the power of this 'imagining'. In our day-dreams or visualisations, we are creating. We are setting a frequency to an idea or a happening and filling that happening in with emotion and detail. Once set, we send that vibration out into the world and if we are receptive to what we have imagined, we are likely to receive back from our environment happenings or occurrences matching that frequency.

This is true with good or negative imaginings. The young man who daydreams of owning his own fabulous car and sees himself driving it down streets he knows, while waving to his friends is well on the way to realizing that 'dream', simply through the act of visualising that outcome complete with emotion and joy.

Also, the elderly woman who worries constantly about her house being burgled and stays awake at night running through all the worst-case scenarios is well on her way to bringing to herself that nightmare experience. And no she doesn't create the burglar but if there happens to be one about, her own fear and worry over such things will put her home on the top of the list for a matching experience to the one she has been visualizing in her worrying.

Think of the pineal gland as the connection point of the invisible satellite dish we are born with (or develop somewhere along the way) and that connection point is both where we receive and broadcast information.

The information is received there and then flows into whatever programme we have developed for interpretation of that information – so clairaudients will 'hear' the information in some intelligible form as the information flows through their auditory system. Clairvoyants will interpret that information through their visual cortex, although there may be no substance or form reflecting light in the outer world to be 'seen'.

You could then possibly say that what is 'seen' or 'heard' is imagined, but the information that prompted the imagination to REAL-ise the vision or the sounds is very real.

When you envisage a wanted experience your pineal gland likewise translates that imagined scenario into frequency and emits that frequency out into being – which then finds its match out in the world and draws a matching experience.

One of the most powerful survival tools for the sixth is to get a handle on this process and instead of being an open receiver 24/7 of random impressions and information is to tune themselves to a desired frequency and practice emitting that frequency as much as possible. In this way, the outward channel becomes stronger and can drown out all the input of any frequency lower than what is being emitted.

SO focusing on love, delight – even contentment; appreciating beauty and harmony, actively looking for things to appreciate and EN-joy, this keeps your invisible satellite emitting the frequency of positive uplifting experience and for the most part drowns out all frequencies which are weaker. Of course should a significant negative experience take place a short way away or should a loved one send up an energetic flare – this would still be received, just not the depression of the neighbour or the sadness of the little girl down the road.

It's your satellite dish – and you get to choose what purpose it will serve.

There are hundreds of memes out there of empaths wearing armour simply to participate in public and in truth, a raw unshielded empath – no matter their channel of translation – will experience crowded public spaces like that classic strobe light death metal torture.

However if we harness the technique of setting a frequency – love, joy, curiosity, appreciation – and amplify that – then going out into public can be rather like nymphs walking before us strewing rose-petals in our path and singing gentle melodies. People will want to interact with us not knowing why? Cashiers will smile and store clerks will compete to assist us – because what we are broadcasting feels good to everyone around us when we feel good.

The same is true in reverse – the six sensed often discover this ability by accident and when they are in a foul mood – just about everyone around them gets hammered with radiating spiked energy that brings to them the worst kind of experiences, which further infuriate them.

Fortunately the blowback from harming another soul is a flip-switch built into the six-sensed that most often stops us dead in our tracks and is the simple reason that many of us are kind and nice most of the time. If we are not – we get to experience the pain, disappointment and sadness of others that we cause; personally. This can turns us into 'people-pleasers', as we prefer to share in the positive emotions of others rather than less pleasant ones – especially when we are the cause.

The Celtic Wiccan belief holds a parallel understanding – that activating a negative intent on another will rebound 10 times on the sender – and in that way they moderate their own thoughts and intentions. The six-sensed live this energetic reality which can either mandate kindness and gentleness or lead to extreme emotional chaos as we reel through our days sending out daggers and trying to dodge the 10 returning ones, feeling victimized and out of control in these natural ebbs and flows.

We have not really begun to understand how the sixth sense works, not with any kind of scientific certainty. What we have is the experience of those few six-sensed that have managed to harness their sense positively – but even the experience of others is limited in its value when it comes to receiving and translating incoming information.

Imagine for a moment a library, on the shelves and displayed on the walls in pictures are all of your life experiences. Your understandings of life and your assumptions on everything. It is here in this library that your legion – your highest self and all those souls in the next world focused on your well-being (be they Ancestors, souls with incomplete experiences sticking around to complete their own lessons in various areas or souls passionate about areas of life you are exploring) are gathered.

So here in the library of you is a gathering of well-meaning souls focused on supporting you in living your best life.

And let us say that on this occasion, they wish to express to you that a new home is awaiting you and you are about to encounter a doorway to the new home you have been broadcasting your desire for.

In this library there are no general compendiums of meaning or psychic translation guides, there are just your own beliefs, experiences and understandings of life.

In this life-library there is the thread of a theme. Every time you have been about to change homes or find a new home, you have seen a certain type of bird – a Raven perhaps, flying overhead.

So your legion arranges for you such a sighting to express to you the imminence of the new home but instead of trusting your own experience with this sighting, you look up online the meaning of seeing a raven fly overhead. This is where it all goes wrong.

Instead of trusting that your legion is working with your own personal compendium of experiences and understandings – you are now thrown into chaos with one source offering that Ravens mean luck, another saying death is imminent and the message – that you felt the import of when you received it - gets garbled.

Our people (I call them our faeries) or our higher self (or spirit-self) is communicating with us in our own internal language and only we can ever truly understand the meaning of the impressions we receive from spirit.

As mediums when we see clients, by not understanding this we can lose so much in translation.

Once with a particularly sceptical friend, a woman made a forceful energetic appearance to me wanting me to pass on to him the assurance that she was with him and was supporting his efforts in this world. She knew keenly that describing her to him would not convince him of her presence and so she showed me an odd looking device – certainly nothing I had ever seen before. After many minutes of describing the device, he knew without doubt who she was as one of his grandmothers had treasured this old butter churn and he had never seen its like anywhere else. I'd never seen one at all so could only describe what I saw. To me it looked rather like a brass concrete mixer but if I had concluded that then the whole message would have been lost.

When receiving messages for others we will often not understand the importance of the message or be able to translate it for them. All we can do is present as cleanly and accurately as possible, the imagery, sound or impressions we receive and allow the recipient to find for themselves the meaning therein.

In trusting our own intuition therefore, it is vital we reference first and foremost the library of our own experience. If a Raven means happy times to us, then that is what is being conveyed – not whatever someone else has decided that means.

There is not a single compendium of meaning for humanity and so every message, every intuition is tailor-made for our own interpretation. And its also okay if we don't get the meaning right away. Perhaps we will understand it in retrospect and every such experience will gain us more confidence in interpreting what we are receiving.

Staying clear of other people's assumptions and interpretations is vital. Trial and error is the best path forward as we try to create a dialogue with our supporters. The older Ancestors for example can be vastly challenging. Not only does their language sometimes differ so much from our present day language but their imagery also can seem quite foreign.

A dear friend with Native American ancestry always presents a challenge as his people lay out implements and totems for him which have great spiritual significance to them, but are meaningless to him. It is always an adventure to research each image to piece together a message – like playing Pictionary with the dearly departed only they lived in such a different time that none of their pictures are common to life in today.

Being willing to NOT know what something means has been one of my greatest lessons in translating for others. Even for my own self, images and messages received (sometimes even in dreams) seem unintelligible at first. So I've learned to write them down and mostly, in time, the meaning will become clear. Sometimes it will take a long time but looking back at the message you will know exactly what you were being told in that moment.

Whether you are receiving or emitting information there can be no doubt that you are in a dialogue with life. Information received from your environment or from your supporters can support and assist you in your daily life and if that becomes overwhelming, you can learn to broadcast signal through the same portal that will bring to you more of whatever frequency you broadcast.

If every six-sensed individual in every part of the world spent a single day in appreciation and delight and broadcast that frequency powerfully through their day, we could shift this world in a single day to a higher frequency and a kinder experience. We have that power.

But as long as we curl up in self-isolation, being battered by the impressions we receive all day, unwilling to own our abilities and afraid of their rejection by normals, we are only helping to amplify the fear and trauma that has overrun the earth.

That's not to say we are to blame for any of it – but its certainly not what we came here for. We didn't come here to sponge up negative emotion or tranquillise and numb ourselves, we came here to harness our ability to amplify joy and peace, for ourselves first through adventure and play – and then naturally as a consequence of our own alignment with our well-being – amplify positive momentum out into the world and change it forever.

As one of Marianne Williamson's legion inspired her to write:

"Our deepest fear is not that we are inadequate. Our deepest fear is that we are powerful beyond measure. It is our Light, not our Darkness, that most frightens us".

This feels especially true for the six-sensed who have not even begun to scratch the surface of the depth and breadth of their abilities.

In this age, all six-sensed are needed – as whole and healed as they can be – literally to save the world from being swallowed by the shadows of fear, doubt and chaos.

Will you be counted as one of the souls who chose love, joy and prosperity and lived your best and most inspired life – while at the same time uplifting and inspiring others merely through your presence? Or will you hide your light under the covers of self-doubt and fear of rejection and watch this age go by in self-imposed isolation and fear?

This is your time. Don't let it go by without your active and joyous participation.

Mediumship

The information we are receiving through our sixth sense is sometimes from the collective human consciousness, sometimes from our environment and sometimes it's from a soul that lives now beyond the veil of human existence – what most call 'the next world'.

If each band of frequencies represents a 'world' – then there may be endless worlds through which we, as spiritual beings, grow and develop. I believe there are only two real 'directions' of our journey, towards 'the light' and away from it. If we keep ourselves focused TOWARDS 'the light', maintaining a high as possible frequency, then only communication or information that moves us in that direction or comes from that direction can reach us.

It is those living unconscious lives, ping-ponging back and forth in response to material realities, who are vulnerable to ill-influences – more than any six-sensed individual at any point along their journey.

I'm not saying there are no ill intentioned momentum's out there. There are. But these are around human beings acting in ways that are deprived of goodness or truth.

I have never met or experienced an ill-intentioned soul from the next world.

It simply cannot be.

We are Beings of spirit, having a human experience – at the end of which we emerge completely back into our spiritual reality, with all we have learned and know from here. That spiritual reality is 'light', and that same light gives life to the world.

It is the human experience that opens the conscious choice of 'towards' or 'away from' the light, and so only this experience allows the choice to get lost in shadows.

Eudaemonic Resonance – the impulse towards 'more' and 'better' and 'whole' or 'happy', will always be calling us towards higher and higher frequencies through what feels good to us. Always.

Discussions I have with others around mediumship often boil down to the fear of 'possession' or some version of that but I promise you, if you nurture a relationship with Source, God if you're okay with that word or the Good of the Universe, you will always enjoy the protection of knowing when something is on the path to joy and better.

To be a six-sensed human living through this human experience consciously, aware of the life all around you, aware of frequency and vibration and always allowing GOOD, there is nothing on that journey that can harm you – besides other humans with ill-intent and you will feel those coming a mile away.

Those individuals that surrender to shadow, get mired in ill-intent, they are not IN the next world, and so cannot be communicating with anyone from there. That said, as I outlined before, you never need to experience those in the next world at all in this human experience.

Its entirely your choice how you receive and interpret the information through your sixth sense.

The God-thing

Alright you dear souls, taking a deep breath lets dive into this sticky one for a moment from a fresh perspective:

Forget for a moment all the conflicting history, your own aversions or biases, and lets look at this logically, taking energetic existence and frequency into account.

Lets agree that the most beautifully crafted and sculpted table, can never know the carpenter who lovingly made it. The wood of that table, that once was a magnificent tree and is now a beautiful work of art, exists at a certain frequency of Being and it just cant grasp or even be aware of, anything above the band-width it lives within.

Its experience – while alive – was limited to that single bandwidth, a measure of frequency that all other living trees also share.

Exchange that sample for a painting, a flower or any created thing and the analogy rings true.

All life exists within a band-width, a frequency of experience and dealing with everything that shows up on its own bandwidth is usually enough life to be getting on with.

The bandwidth within which the five-sensed experience life is therefore narrower to the experience of the six-sensed as we get to experience life from the hard and seemingly solid right up to the energetic, or spiritual – whereas their experience for the most part does not include energetic frequencies.

In our own experience we have affirmation of this. You will remember times when you were really high-frequency, when life was GOOD, when you were in joy or even just contentment. From there, life feels sweet, colours brighter, perception sharper. As we elevate, we have access to information and experiences on higher frequencies. Logical right?

I've mentioned the dearly departed, and how they are all out there, in the next or the next bandwidth of energy, in a higher level of frequency, and if we tune in, we can have contact with them – but even they, from that higher frequency, do not know all of what lies ahead of them as they elevate.

Five-sensed beings have no experience of the next bandwidths of existence, its our sixth sense that makes experiencing those higher frequencies possible.

SO really, mankind would have no idea at all of what lies beyond this earth or what exists at higher and higher vibrational frequencies, were it not for remarkable individuals that have appeared to every tribe in every region throughout history.

To name but a few of these, whose writings and works still exist in some form today, there was Abraham, Krishna, Buddha, Zoroaster, Moses, Christ, Mohammed, The Bab and Baha'u'llah. Without exception these 'teachers' all spoke of two ideas; of Divine Intelligence and to treat each other as we would like to be treated.

Were it not for them (and the others whose teachings have been lost to time), we would have no idea that there IS a Higher intelligence or a Source, or a Creator. The language changes from group to group but if we are all tables, these Messengers all spoke of a Carpenter.

So there was some Divine Intelligence that stepped out of the ebb and flow of what we know of as life, to download to multiple individuals through the passage of time, the information that there IS a Higher Power, and be kind to one another (and heaps of other useful guidance, some specifically for that time and some that would apply throughout time).

That tells me that we would not have gotten there on our own – even with a LOT of time and even if we got VERY clever, because we simply cant see beyond that horizon of experience.

However, if you KNOW that there is a Source of creation – even at a frequency that you may never reach high enough to experience in the human journey, you CAN reach upwards in frequency simply by focusing directly in the 'direction' of that highest frequency. That 'direction', not being a physical but an energetic thing, feels like appreciation, love, joy or awe. So in any of those feelings, we are already reaching 'upward'.

And remember, we think in terms of space and time but in terms of frequency, all can exist in the same space – just at multiple vibrational levels. So Source can be right here, right now, just at an incredibly elevated frequency – and if we reach 'upward' in that direction, our being will be elevated simply in response to that focus,

Its not the teachings of the Messengers or Teachers that are so different, rather the capacity of the people they were speaking to and the time and place they arrived in that is so different.

The six-sensed have immense capacity in this area, mostly unexplored, so we don't know what we can achieve when we combine the six-sensed experience with a focus on Divine Intelligence, but it feels like it will be an exciting adventure to find out!

Let us bear in mind, that any souls in the next bandwidth of experience, or the 'next world' as its often called, are also limited, They are further along the journey 'upwards', to be sure, but they are not boundless in their own present ambit of Being. Unless they are one of the souls that have reached the Source, and been designated as emissaries or been sent on particular missions, all other dearly departed ones have their limitations. That's not to say that they don't hold vast wisdom on matters below their frequency, but it would perhaps not be wise to count on their knowledge of anything 'above' them.

To stretch the beautifully crafted table analogy, that would be like the table asking the lace tablecloth about the carpenter.

Exploring frequency, receptivity and understanding then: Have you ever read a book that inspired you or elevated you, and then you returned to that book decades later? And then upon rereading it, found a whole new layer of information wound around that first that you just cant believe you didn't GET the first time? Really good books are like that, they have dimensions within them that you can never fully grasp at the first read.

As you grow, as your perception widens and deepens, your frequency elevates, and from that new perspective, new truths become discernable. The book doesn't change, but your capacity for the information in them does. Truth, love and trust, wisdom or knowing also needs to be received.

All the writings of Great Teachers are like that, you can return to them at different times and get whole new swathes of insight from them.

Mankind might only have been ready for parables and exemplar stories at one point, but grew in capacity as time rolled forward. But we can still revisit those stories now and from our understanding here, they can still hold great wisdom.

However, without humanity having been TOLD that there were infinitely higher frequencies and that at the highest there was Divine Intelligence, we might never have known that.

Mankind has made a mess of the messages from this Source. It harnesses them to pit people against each other and harness resources and assert power. True. But if you ignore the behaviour of Humans for a moment, and take a step back and observe the sequence of Teachers that have appeared on the earth every 500 to 1000 years, it seems that there might be a Divine Hand in all of this. And if that is true, then the teachings of these Teachers – in as authentic and unaltered form as you can find them, might offer guidance for our intellectual minds to chew on.

I'm okay with the God-word and I love all the pathways to 'Light' that make humans happier, more joyful and kinder. There are in my experience deep wells of wisdom to be found everywhere.

Each of us will find a path that speaks to us, that resonates for us and brings us comfort. In my personal experience, developing a personal relationship with Divine Intelligence is the best of all choices. Have chats – Lightward. Reach for love, and then from a place of a deep personal connection, find a spiritual path or practice that works for you, that is comfortable, that is welcoming and that inspires you. Reassess everyday if needed, but don't let the behaviour of historical greedy humans deprive you of benefiting from the wisdom that has been injected into the history of mankind from these Messengers.

The phrase "I'm spiritual but not religious" is an oxymoron. All these teachers through time – that were the source of what we today call 'religion', came to open for mankind portals to higher vibrational frequencies that are in themselves, the realms of spirit. Were it not for the religious icons, we would know nothing OF Spirit at all.

If we are to be NOT something, let it be not prejudiced, not bigoted and not elitist. As the Sufi poet Rumi has said: "We are all just walking each other home".

Our paths may all be different, and that's Okay. As long as we cause no harm on our journey (intentional harm that is), lets give everyone the space to explore spirit individually and independently, and then celebrate the common ground we find between us.

The Divine Intelligence I have experience of doesn't need us to be, but loved us INTO BE-ing anyway and that knowing can uplift and support our journeys – just as it is, even if you adorn it with no robes and no mantles.

What mankind has made a mess of does not need to be an obstacle to YOUR connection to Source. As a six-sensed being you are uniquely able to explore the realms of spirit in ways that can enhance your human experience tremendously and there is great comfort and support to be experienced in an individual connection to Divine Intelligence – even if communication from that Source filters through intermediaries lower down the rungs of frequency to reach us here, on the edge of light, dancing with shadow.

Is the future AI or IA?

As an active empathic six-sensed Indigo Adult, no longer shunning or hiding from my extra-sensory self, 'normals' feel to me like furniture or solid (moving) obstacles. Out in the world as I go about my days they seldom register on my radar as anything but an obstacle to be navigated. Their vibrational reality feels the same as inanimate objects – so focused are they on this physical 'reality' that they have lowered their own vibration to become one with it.

And yet any one of those beings, perhaps in times of crisis or in a moment of love – can elevate themselves back to their intended state (intended from the perspective of their spirit self manifesting into human form for the joy, wonder and awe that is possible here) and take their place in the light.

Others of them – usually through shame, blame or some perceived or real 'unforgivable sin' have cut themselves off forever from their true spiritual self and therefore in truth are animated 'objects'.

When the connection with the true self is severed, so is the connection to Source, to healing, to vitality, to passion and joy and so these beings must scramble about in the dust for substitutes. So they muck about in depravity, seeking deepening depths of darkness as the only 'feelings' available to them are now the attractions of the flesh and dirt.

This explanation can sound very biblical and is thrown about like a whip of judgement by those trying to frighten people back to the light – but I have no personal opinions either way.

We manifested into this human realm for joy, for the thrill and discovery of co-creation. We were created in the image of our creator and we therefore share unimaginable potential as creators and attractors of beauty and joy.

We were also given choice. Divine free will is a protected right of all of human creation and it's not for any of us to judge another's choices.

When spiritual beings who have manifested human forms to delight in this realm of being go wrong – they can go badly wrong and I believe that there is a point of wrongness where their higher selves, what we know of as our spiritual reality steps away from its created manifestation.

Like the robotics creator that disowns its murderous rampaging robot that has strayed outside of its intended purpose. This would be a point quite far down the path of shadow but it would need to happen when the human form steps so far away from the light of spirit and grows to hate the light and actively and with considered intent acts against the light and therefore can never be returned to the light.

Science will need to delve this reality in future – when a human form so entirely cuts itself off from its spiritual true self in an irreversible series of choices bourn out of hatred for all that is 'good'.

Of course those forms would need to seek out alternative sustenance of this world. Chemical or alchemical, these human forms have identified themselves entirely with this physical reality and so seek to extend their lives here through whatever means necessary – without conscience. I believe this is what adrenochrome is truly intended for.

But our purpose in this world is not about this world. We came here only to experience the Laws and Forces of the Universe in the most tangible form possible. To learn about them, and find our place amongst them.

We are sparks of Divine Truth on a journey back to the Source of all being and that journey can be joyful and full of delight. Following our purpose through our individual expression through particular sets of DNA with differing Ancestral inspiration and unique channels of accessing truth and inspiration should make this world a garden of dancing, celebrating and exalting forms connected as much as possible and as fully as is feasible to our spiritual reality.

Instead, there have been those who for so long have denied themselves or denied the truth of our spiritual reality and become so focused on this plane of existence that they have cut themselves off from source and imagine themselves competitors with the light for the allegiance of the mass of humanity.

But the Indigo Adults can no more be cut from Source as a bird could be from its wings and still be called a bird. We feel our reality AS Source, as sparks of source flung out across the vibrational universe to play, to learn and to expand the reach of light and we feel that calling in our bones. It is our truth and our torment – when nothing we hear or see in this reality affirms for us the acceptance of our true nature. We struggle fiercely – not with the world but with all the wrongness we see, feel and know is present in the world as it is today.

We struggle with our own knowing and we struggle to be authentic in a world that seeks to douse the flame of who we are. But a better world is coming, and we who overcome – that survive that struggle, are a significant part of the world that will take the place of this one.

In the simplest terms, through acceptance of our reality on the leading edge of human evolution, we embrace our true six-sensed nature and take the step out of gloom into Truth and align with our true selves, we become lights in the darkness of a world that has been nudged persistently, over a long time – into darkness of spiritual ignorance.

Our spiritual reality IS the truth of ourselves and all that is joyful, delighted and loving IS our intended natural state. Anything outside of the scope of those truths is an aberration of the intention for the human experience.
Love IS the force that binds frequencies that match together. Some have called this the Law of Attraction but this Law, this force, is quite simply LOVE. It binds the elements of the atoms, holds the stars in their place and allows all of what we know as existence.

Unconditional love is a term that has been greatly misunderstood. To LOVE, unconditionally simply means to align with love, be guided BY love and stand rooted IN love – both for ourselves and for all of existence. Since it is at the root of our very existence, love is often the easiest essence to tune into, sometimes by thinking of a person or a process for which we have great love. If we can find and tune into that love, just the love itself, we align ourselves with the force of life that allows and surrounds all life and then the operation of Eudaemonic resonance is assured, that we will be inexorably drawn forward by that love to better and better lives.

There are those I love dearly, many of whom are now beyond the human experience, and when I think of them, I feel filled with love and well-being. Bring love into any situation and it will 'turn the lights on' in any dark room and ease the path forward for all involved. This is the true expression of unconditional love, standing IN LOVE, regardless of the surrounding conditions. If enough of us tune into love, in its purest form, we could transform the path of humanity overnight.

This age is the first time in human history that those of us in clear and confident acknowledgement of our extra senses have been 'allowed' – by average social standards to live free and UN-persecuted lives and that's not even true everywhere yet but those of us that CAN step out of the shadows, if we have the courage to follow our authentic selves, will make room for others to do the same.

Our sixth senses are not infallible, we are not a legion of prophets. We are merely able to sense more – truth and untruth stand naked before us, right and wrong are clear for us. But as we explore our abilities, we must remain humble. Yes, we have connections to greater truths, we have access to beings who have passed on with vast knowledge, but all received information is filtered through our own perceptions, decisions and personal biases and that step is vastly flawed.

The best and clearest of us are those that have cleared themselves as much as possible of our own garbage. The detritus of human conditioning and ancestral misunderstandings.

A beautiful prayer that relates to this ideal state comes from the Writings of Baha'u'llah that asks simply of the Creator to "make of me a hollow reed through which your love may flow" – anything less than that and the light gets coloured, tainted, misunderstood and so we are not all-knowing but rather more-knowing.

The 'normals' who currently own most of the world's 'stuff' fear most our discernment of truth as societies manipulators have made of this world a dust-heap of lies and perception that even our fledgling Indigo children can see through. When you live in a world constructed primarily of lies our mere existence frightens them, but they know that we are afraid to speak out, afraid to acknowledge the source of our knowing and unsure of ourselves – so they still have time. How long they truly have is up to each of us.

Most significant will be the shift of the evolution of mankind from artificial intelligence (required only by those disconnected from spirit and therefore only able to expand through artificial means) to the truth-centred expansive and delightful evolution into a world that embraces truth, authenticity and spiritual reality and brings about the marriage of science with spirit to forge ahead into new and sublime levels of existence for the human experience.

We came here for joy, what we found was suffering, sure. But we came here – simply through the authentic exploration of our innate capabilities and our access to expanded knowing – to bring light back to the human experience and return it to its rightful place as a step along the evolution of spirit full of play, joy and delightful learning.

So yes, that means we did not choose for ourselves an easy path. Try for a moment thinking as your higher vibrational true self – standing at the portal to the human experience do you think you would have chosen the door marked "Simple but low stress, minimal impact" or the door marked "Highest difficulty highest rewards"? I know enough of myself to not doubt for a moment what my choice will always be no matter what frequency of life I'm living on. All or nothing – I'm IN!

And in that moment, we KNEW that no matter what the social construct or the domestic environment we manifested into we COULD overcome anything because we would be connected to all those who had gone before and their love and guidance would sustain us.

Our greatest danger was being convinced to disconnect ourselves from our extra senses – through shame or a desire for acceptance because only there, in that deadly quiet, that forlorn stillness, are we ever truly left feeling alone and that loneliness has driven so many of us to hop off of this moral coil and back to our spiritual reality. I don't judge that choice. There were times in my life when I too came close to making the final decision.

But if you are reading this you did not. You stayed and you still hold all the potential of your authentic Indigo self and with it the power to effect change in the world. And there is no knocking on doors or immersing yourself in the ick of this world necessary. All that is needed for our generation of Indigos to succeed in righting the direction of the world is to go inward, nurture ourselves, learn about our capacities – humbly and in full knowledge that this is a new area of exploration and we need to remain open to new understandings of truth.

Connect, meditate, read, learn. Deepen ourselves in truths that feel GOOD when we hear them and allow our internal guidance towards joy, peace and delight to guide us to true fulfilment of our purpose. Keep questioning everything and carve out a life for yourself enhanced by your legions of supporters and guides.

Understand that initially you will misunderstand, misinterpret impressions and 'downloads' but keep exploring your ability to receive clearly. Find tools and teachers that help you through your next steps and move on when you outgrow them. Trust YOURSELF to know your own next steps and relearn what it feels like to live effortlessly. No 'musts' 'should' or 'coulds', just be in what IS and let the lightness of yay, yummy and yes! guide you forward.

We ARE the next step in the ever advancing civilization of mankind and if you've been living under a blanket hiding your true self, it is time to let your light shine.
And as you do that, your connection to and momentum toward all that is good and true will create waves that will draw others along with you – with no effort from you. You will be a beacon for emitting glimmers of grace out into the world, just through your own example. As you elevate the vibration of your being those around you will not be able to help being elevated with you.

This is true, authentic expansion of the light – an expansion that comes from within and radiates outward effortlessly. When you do this the dishonesty of manipulation and fakery will fall away and mankind will soar on the wings of true freedom and unlimited potential.

You chose this path and at one point you KNEW you had it in you to succeed. If you've doubted yourself, it was only the whisperings of the shadow-filled world that overcame your confidence. Reclaim your true destiny now and your life CAN be a dance of joy and delight from here on. It has been your denial of your true nature that has kept you mourning in the shadows but now you are free. You are accepted, acknowledged, and so vastly and delightedly loved.

Know and be your truth self. All goodness and beauty flows from that.

Acknowledgements

With sincere thanks to Kevin, for being a melodious sounding-board. To Ron and Rene for editorial input an encouragement and special thanks to all my clients and students, who present me with opportunities to serve, and to delve deeper, everyday.

To you dear reader, for taking a chance on this work, in the hope of finding some ease, peace or clarity; if it has provided even a moments peace, a slight shift to ease and hope, then this work will have hit its mark. Thanks to all who left reviews and brought this work into your world.

And to ensure that others may also be lead to challenge some limiting perceptions, be offered some ease, could I ask that you take a moment to go along to
www.books2read.com
or to whichever platform you found this work, and leave a review.
It is with reviews that the computer systems decide whether or not to show this
work to others, and so these few minutes of your time will make a meaningful impact to getting this work out to those who could be consoled, enlivened or eased by the perspectives documented here.

My part of this is done, its success is in your hands now.

Thank you for all you do, out here on this leading edge. You courageous soul YOU!

Alyce Dylan

About Alyce:

Alyce Dylan has been a successful businesswoman and international Public Speaker and now serves her clients and students as a Coach, Intuitive Counsellor, Veteran Traditional Reiki Master and thriving Indigo Adult.

The perspectives that have eased and supported her journey are those she shares with her clients and students to enable them to thrive at this accelerated growth-point of the human experience.

Having travelled across the globe, speaking on ethical business models and their role in healthy societies, she now once again takes this message out to the world, in the knowledge that through empowering and strengthening Indigo Adults, Children and the six-sensed, HSP's and Intuitives, we can speed our journey towards a healthy and prosperous world.

https://www.facebook.com/askalyce9999

More from Alyce Dylan:

Along with this work Alyce has also made available various journals and guided workbooks including:

Me (My little book of Self-Actualisation)
DezynALife
and **Man.Kind.**

Not all of which were available on the day of launch of this work, so please sign up at Books2Read for notification of the release dates of these works.

Currently in process is a work for men, celebrating the male journey to self-actualisation and looking at the role of partners in that journey.

Milton Keynes UK
Ingram Content Group UK Ltd.
UKHW030745221024
449869UK00001B/64